Skills Practice
Workbook

**Level 2
Book 2**

McGraw Hill SRA

Columbus, OH

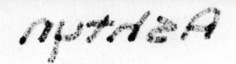

SRAonline.com

 SRA

Send all inquiries to this address:
SRA/McGraw-Hill
4400 Easton Commons
Columbus, OH 43219-6188

ISBN: 978-0-07-610477-2
MHID: 0-07-610477-X

9 QDB 13 12 11

The **McGraw-Hill** Companies

Table of Contents

Unit 4 Look Again

Lesson 1
Phonics:
/ōō/ spelled oo. 1
Word Structure:
Plurals, Synonyms and Antonyms 3
Selection Vocabulary 5
Comprehension:
Main Idea and Details 7
Inquiry:
Charts 9
Writing:
Explaining How Something Happens 11
Spelling:
/ōō/ spelled oo. 13
Grammar:
Pronouns 15

Lesson 2
Phonics:
/ōō/ spelled u, u_e, _ew, _ue 17
Word Structure:
Compound Words and Contractions 19
Selection Vocabulary 21
Inquiry:
Making Observations. 23
Writing:
Writing a Persuasive Paragraph 25
Spelling:
/ōō/ spelled u, u_e, _ew, _ue 27
Grammar:
Possessive Pronouns and Nouns 29

Lesson 3
Phonics:
/oo/ spelled oo. 31
Word Structure:
Prefix dis- 33
Selection Vocabulary 35

Writing:
Writing a Book Report 37
Spelling:
/oo/ spelled oo. 39
Grammar:
Conjunctions and Compound Sentences 41

Lesson 4
Phonics:
/ow/ spelled ow, ou_. 43
Word Structure:
Prefixes mis-, mid- 45
Selection Vocabulary 47
Comprehension:
Classify and Categorize. 49
Writing:
Writing a Folktale. 51
Spelling:
/ow/ spelled ow, ou_. 53
Grammar:
Synonyms and Antonyms. 55

Lesson 5
Phonics:
Review /ōō/, /oo/, /ow/ 57
Word Structure:
Inflectional and Comparative Endings,
Irregular Plurals. 59
Selection Vocabulary 61
Inquiry:
Types of Camouflage. 63
Writing:
Writing a Make-Believe Story 65
Spelling:
Review /ōō/, /oo/, /ow/ 67
Grammar:
Colons 69

Unit 5 Courage

Lesson 1

Phonics:
/aw/ spelled *aw, au_*. 71
Word Structure:
Suffixes *-er, -ness* 73
Selection Vocabulary 75
Inquiry:
Interview. 77
Spelling:
/aw/ spelled *aw, au_*. 79
Grammar:
Capitals and Commas in Letter
Greetings/Closings 81
Writing:
Poetry (Riddle) 83

Lesson 2

Phonics:
/aw/ spelled *augh, ough, all, al* 85
Word Structure:
Suffixes *-ly, -y, -ed* 87
Selection Vocabulary 89
Comprehension:
Cause and Effect. 91
Inquiry:
Brave People. 93
Spelling:
/aw/ spelled *augh, ough, all, al* 95
Grammar:
Quotation Marks 97
Writing:
Poetry (Acrostic Poem). 99

Lesson 3

Phonics:
ough sound/spelling 101
Word Structure:
Suffixes *-less, -ful*; Prefixes and Suffixes as
Syllables 103
Selection Vocabulary 105
Writing:
Poetry (Rhyming Poem) 107

Spelling:
Contrast Sound/Spellings for *ough* 109
Grammar:
Commas in Dialogue 111

Lesson 4

Phonics:
/oi/ spelled *oi, _oy* 113
Word Structure:
Homographs and Homophones. 115
Selection Vocabulary 117
Comprehension:
Sequence 119
Writing:
News Story. 121
Spelling:
/oi/ spelled *oi, _oy* 123
Study Skills:
Using a Dictionary, a Glossary, and
a Thesaurus 125
Grammar:
Adverbs 127

Lesson 5

Phonics:
/aw/ and /oi/. 129
Word Structure:
Related Words, Word Families 131
Selection Vocabulary 133
Comprehension:
Author's Purpose. 135
Writing:
Play 137
Spelling:
/aw/ and /oi/. 139
Grammar:
Verb Tenses 141

Unit 6 America's People

Lesson 1

Phonics:
Contrast /ū/ and /ow/, /o͞o/ and
/ū/, /o͞o/ and /oo/ 143
Word Structure:
Antonyms, Synonyms, Compound Words,
Contractions 145
Selection Vocabulary 147
Comprehension:
Fact and Opinion 149
Writing:
Personal Letter 151
Spelling:
Contrast /ō/ and /ow/, /o͞o/
and/ū/, /o͞o/ and /oo/ 153
Grammar:
Noun, Verb, Subject, and Predicate Review . . 155

Lesson 2

Phonics:
Silent Consonants 157
Word Structure:
Prefixes *dis-, un-, mis-* and *mid-* 159
Selection Vocabulary 161
Comprehension:
Cause and Effect 163
Inquiry 165
Writing:
Personal Letter 167
Spelling:
Silent Letters 169
Study Skills:
Using an Encyclopedia 171
Grammar:
Capitalization, End Marks,
Complete/Incomplete Sentences Review . . 173

Lesson 3

Phonics:
Three-Letter Consonant Blends 175
Word Structure:
Inflectional and Comparative Endings,
Suffixes *-er, -ness* 177
Selection Vocabulary 179

Writing:
Formal Letter 181
Spelling:
Three-Letter Consonant Blends 183
Study Skills:
Use Multiple Sources 185
Grammar:
Capitalization, Noun, Adjectives,
Articles Review 187

Lesson 4

Phonics:
/ow/ and /aw/ 189
Word Structure:
Suffixes *-ly, -y, -less,* and *-ful* 191
Selection Vocabulary 193
Writing:
Writing a Realistic Story 195
Spelling:
Contrast /aw/ and /ow/ 197
Study Skills:
Using Newspapers and Magazines 199
Grammar:
Subject/Verb Agreement, Commas in
a Series, Contractions Review 201

Lesson 5

Phonics:
/aw/, /ow/, /o͞o/, /oo/, /ū/, and /ō/ sounds,
Silent Letters, Three-Letter Blends 203
Word Structure:
Homographs, Homophones, Related Words,
Word Families 205
Selection Vocabulary 207
Comprehension:
Drawing Conclusions 209
Writing:
Writing a Biography 211
Spelling:
Review 213
Study Skills:
Using New Technology 215
Grammar:
Compound, Imperative Sentences, Colons,
Synonyms, Antonyms 217

Name _____ **Date** _____

/ōō/ Sound/Spellings

Focus   The /ōō/ sound can be spelled oo.

Practice   **Read the sentence. Change the word in the box to make a new rhyming word. Write the new word on the blank line.**

1. | **broom** | The bride and _____ had a fancy wedding.

2. | **moon** | We usually eat our lunch at _____.

3. | **noodle** | Aunt Jenny got a _____ from the pet store.

4. | **pool** | The soup has to _____ before we eat it.

5. | **mood** | Pepperoni pizza is Henry's favorite _____.

6. | **boots** | A plant has _____ that hold it in the ground.

7. | **gloom** | Many flowers _____ in the springtime.

8. | **poof** | I heard the raindrops hitting the _____ during the thunderstorm.

UNIT 4 **Lesson 1**

 **Apply** **Pick a word from the box below to complete each sentence. Write the word on the blank line.**

moon	scoop	bedroom	loose	boots
cartoons	zoomed	tools	pool	too

1. I can see the stars from my _____ window.

2. A mechanic uses _____ to repair cars.

3. On Saturday mornings I enjoy watching _____ on TV.

4. The rocket _____ straight up to the sky.

5. My dentist said I have a tooth that is _____.

6. Tonya ate a small _____ of mashed potatoes with her dinner.

7. The cowboy had a spur on each of his _____.

8. Swimming in the _____ on a hot day feels great.

9. Alex wants to join us and play checkers _____.

10. Light from the _____ can help you see on a dark night.

Name _____ Date _____

Plurals

- Adding **–s** or **–es** to a word makes it **plural**.
- **Plural** words show that there is more than one.

Practice Add –s or –es to each word to make it plural. Then write the new word on the blank line.

1. book + s _____

4. costume + s _____

2. trick + s _____

5. marsh + es _____

3. store + s _____

6. glass + es _____

Apply Add –s or –es to the word in parentheses ( ) to complete the sentence. Write the word on the blank line.

1. I use the _____ on my paper to write neatly. (line)

2. Our baseball team has two _____. (coach)

3. Susan made four _____ of cookies for the bake sale. (batch)

4. Emily picked a bouquet of _____. (flower)

Synonyms and Antonyms

Focus
- **Synonyms** are words that are similar in meaning. *Tired* and *sleepy* are synonyms.
- **Antonyms** are words that are opposite in meaning. *Bad* and *good* are antonyms.

Practice **Draw a line to match each word to its *synonym*.**

1. small   **a.** giggle

2. ill   **b.** tiny

3. laugh   **c.** angry

4. mad   **d.** sick

Draw a line to match each word to its *antonym*.

1. happy   **a.** day

2. over   **b.** sad

3. night   **c.** empty

4. full   **d.** under

Name _____ Date _____

Selection Vocabulary

Focus

camouflage: *n.* A disguise that makes something look the same as the area around it.

surroundings: *n.* The area around a person or thing.

patterns: *n.* Plural of **pattern**; the order of colors, shapes, or lines.

pretenders: *n.* Plural of **pretender**; something that makes believe it is something else.

blend: *v.* To mix together so as not to be seen.

mimicry: *n.* The act of copying.

Practice **Write three sentences using at least one of the vocabulary words in each sentence.**

1. _____

_____

2. _____

_____

3. _____

_____

Apply Write the word from the box that matches each definition below.

camouflage	surroundings	patterns
pretenders	blend	mimicry

1. _____ to mix together so as not to be seen

2. _____ something that makes believe it is something else

3. _____ a disguise that makes something look the same as the area around it

4. _____ the act of copying

5. _____ the order of colors, shapes, or lines

6. _____ the area around a person or a thing

Name _____ **Date** _____

Main Idea and Details

- The **main idea** tells what a paragraph is mostly about. A **main idea** sentence gives the main idea of the paragraph. A main idea sentence often comes first in the paragraph to help readers know what the paragraph is about.

- The other sentences in the paragraph give **details** or information about the main idea.

Look through *Animal Camouflage* for main-idea sentences. Write one main-idea sentence below. Then give some details about the main idea.

Page: _____

Main idea sentence: _____

_____

_____

Details about the main idea: _____

_____

_____

_____

Apply **Read the paragraph. It is missing a main-idea sentence. Choose the best main idea sentence from the box and write it on the lines.**

Sometimes animals are too small to defend themselves from harm. Camouflage is a useful tool to help keep them safe. The leaf insect and leafy sea dragon both look like the plants in their surroundings. Both animals even move like the leaves they mimic. Using a disguise keeps these animals alive.

Watching animals out in the wild is exciting.

It is fun to learn about animals.

Animals can use camouflage as protection from predators.

_____

_____

_____

Name _____ Date _____

Charts

Look through "Animal Camouflage" and fill in the chart with information about the animals and how they use camouflage.

Animal Camouflage

Who?	How?	Why?
1.		
2.		
3.		
4.		
5.		

Think about the questions you want to investigate.
Write the title of a chart you could make to help you
with your unit investigation.

_____

_____

_____

Name _____ Date _____

Explaining How Something Happens

Think **Audience: Who** will read your paragraph?

_____

Purpose: What do you want your paragraph to do?

_____

Prewriting Use this graphic organizer to plan your paragraph. In each box, write one step or event. Remember to put the steps in order.

Step		

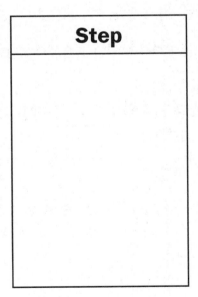
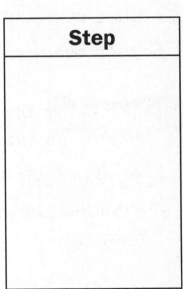

Revising Use this checklist to revise.

☐ Do your sentences describe steps in the correct order?

☐ Did you correctly use time and order words?

☐ Are there facts or details that need to be added?

☐ Are there facts or details that are not needed to explain the process?

Editing/Proofreading Use this checklist to correct mistakes.

☐ Is your paragraph indented?

☐ Is every word or special term spelled correctly?

☐ Does every sentence start with a capital letter?

☐ Does every sentence end with correct punctuation?

Publishing Use this checklist to prepare for publication.

☐ Write or type a neat copy.

☐ Include a drawing or a map that shows the steps in the right order.

Name _____ Date _____

/o͞o/ spelled oo

Focus

- The /o͞o/ sound sounds like the underlined letters in the word m<u>oo</u>.
- One way the /o͞o/ sound can be spelled is *oo*.

Word List

1. hoop
2. tooth
3. mood
4. igloo
5. soon
6. bloom
7. food
8. room
9. pooch
10. pool

Challenge Words

11. noodle
12. rooster
13. school

Practice **Sort the spelling words under the correct heading.**

Write the spelling word that rhymes with the word *zoom:*

1. _____ 2. _____

Write the spelling word that rhymes with the word *loop:*

3. _____

Write the spelling word that ends with the /o͞o/ sound:

4. _____

Write the remaining spelling words on the lines below:

5. _____ 8. _____

6. _____ 9. _____

7. _____ 10. _____

Spelling (continued)

Apply **Proofreading Strategy** Circle the misspelled spelling words. Write the words correctly on the lines below.

Spring is in full blume. Sune, the birds will begin to look for fude to feed their babies, and the pul will open for the season. It really puts me in a good muud!

11. _____

12. _____

13. _____

14. _____

15. _____

Consonant-Substitution Strategy Replace the underlined letter or letters to create a spelling word.

16. _st_oop + h = _____

17. _b_ooth + t = _____

18. _gl_oom + r = _____

19. _sm_ooch + p = _____

Name _____ **Date** _____

Pronouns

Focus

A **pronoun** is a word that takes the place of a noun (person, place, or thing) in a sentence.

Singular Pronouns: I, you, he, she, it, me, him, her
Plural Pronouns: we, they, them, us

Rule	**Examples**
• **Singular nouns** must be replaced with **singular pronouns**.	• **Singular**: The <u>cat</u> thinks **it** can sleep all day.
• **Plural nouns** must be replaced with **plural pronouns**.	• **Plural**: <u>Brianna and Madeline</u> know that **they** are sisters.
• **Pronouns** must also match the **gender** of a noun.	• **Male**: <u>Brian</u> helped **his** family cook breakfast. **Female**: <u>Jennifer</u> read **her** story to the class.

Practice Write a pronoun to replace the underlined noun in each sentence.

1. <u>Jody and I</u> raced our bikes across the park. _____

2. On Saturday, <u>Michael and Anthony</u> went swimming. _____

3. <u>Mom</u> was very surprised with the gifts. _____

4. I saw <u>Brian's</u> poster on the wall. _____

Apply   Circle the *singular pronouns* and underline the *plural pronouns* in the paragraph.

I thought rabbits and hares were the same since they look alike. You wouldn't believe the differences between them. A hare's fur is special. It turns white in the winter. The fur of rabbits changes from brown to grey with the seasons. A mother rabbit will build a nest for her babies, while hares are born on the ground. If we were to see rabbits in the wild they would be with a group, but hares live alone. It has been fun for me to learn about these animals.

Find two sentences in "Hungry Little Hare" that use pronouns. Write each sentence on the blank line and circle the pronoun. Write S above the pronoun if it is singular and P if it is plural.

1. _____

  _____

2. _____

  _____

Name _____ Date _____

/o͞o/ spelled *u, u_e, _ew,* and *_ue*

Focus The /o͞o/ sound is most often spelled with the following patterns: _ew   _ue   u   u_e

Practice Use the following words to fill in the blanks.

ruby	blew	truth	drew	rude
chew	tune	clue	flute	blue

Write the words with the /o͞o/ sound spelled like *grew*.

1. _____   3. _____

2. _____

Write the words with the /o͞o/ sound spelled like *June*.

4. _____   6. _____

5. _____

Write the words with the /o͞o/ sound spelled like *Sue*.

7. _____   8. _____

Write the word with the /o͞o/ sound spelled like *truly*.

9. _____   10. _____

Apply Replace the underlined letter or letters to create a rhyming word. The new word will have the same spelling for the /o͞o/ sound.

1. <u>r</u>ule + m = _____

2. <u>d</u>ew + n = _____

3. <u>bl</u>ue + g = _____

4. <u>c</u>ube + t = _____

5. <u>d</u>rew + g = _____

Read the paragraph. Circle the misspelled words. Write the word correctly on the blanks below. *Hint: Each sentence has one misspelled word.

The Hare and the Tortoise is an old story. One day Tortoise and Hare argue over who is trewly the fastest runner. They decide to have a race to find out the truthe. Each animal just knue Hare would be the winner. Hare took a break and fell asleep by the bloo sprewce tree. Tortoise won the race by using the rewl of staying slow but steady.

1. _____   **4.** _____

2. _____   **5.** _____

3. _____   **6.** _____

Name _____ Date _____

Compound Words

Focus

Compound Words are made when two words are put together to make a new word.

Example
dog + house = doghouse

Practice

Combine the words below to make a *compound word*. Write the compound word on the line.

1. day + dream = _____

2. lady + bug = _____

3. tooth + brush = _____

4. gold + fish = _____

Apply

Fill in the blanks below with a *compound word*.

1. A bath for a bird is a _____.

2. A cloth to put on the table is a _____.

3. A pot to put tea in is a _____.

4. A house for a doll is a _____.

Contractions

Focus

A **contraction** is a shortened form of a pair of words. An apostrophe (') is used to show where a letter or letters have been removed.

Example
here + is = here's

Practice

Read each sentence. Circle the pair of words that form the underlined *contraction*.

1. They're going to see the new giraffe at the zoo.
they have   they are   they will

2. Leslie and Steve wouldn't have a picnic in the rain.
would it   would have   would not

3. Mrs. Carter can't find her purple sweater.
can not   can it   could not

4. She's going to have a ballet lesson today.
she will   she is   she did

5. During art class we'll learn how to draw animals.
we have   we did   we will

6. I've been the classroom helper this week.
I am   I have   I will

7. Johnny thinks it's fun to go camping with his friends.
it is   it will   it did

Name _____ Date _____

Selection Vocabulary

Focus

hare: *n.* A kind of rabbit.

pond: *n.* A small lake.

scent: *n.* A smell.

stump: *n.* The part of a tree that is left after the tree has been cut down.

meadow: *n.* A field of grass.

disguise: *n.* Something that hides the way one looks.

Practice Find the vocabulary words in the word search and circle them. Words can go up, down, or diagonally.

```
S A Y D M N D
C H A R E Z I
E O D M A R S
N R E I D S G
T X P N O N U
H Z O I W O I
D P M O Q I S
F S T U M P E
```

Apply **Fill in each blank with a word from the vocabulary list to complete each sentence.**

1. The _____ of toast filled the air in the kitchen.

2. Tom fed the ducks that were in the _____.

3. A small _____ jumped across the forest path.

4. The detective wore a _____ as he looked for clues.

5. George saw a deer eating in the _____.

6. Squirrels were using the wooden _____ to store nuts.

Write two new sentences using three of the vocabulary words.

1. _____

   _____

2. _____

   _____

Name _____ Date _____

Making Observations

Record the animals you find on your field trip. Describe the place you found the animal. Then tell what the animal looked like. Did it blend into the area around it? Did it look like a tree, limb, or twig? Write your findings in the chart.

Animal	Where I found it	What it looked like

Pick one of the animals you found. Then tell why it was hard or easy to find.

_____

_____

_____

_____

Name _____ Date _____

Writing a Persuasive Paragraph

Think **Audience: Who** will read your persuasive paragraph?

_____

Purpose: What is your reason for writing a persuasive paragraph?

_____

Prewriting **Use this graphic organizer to plan your paragraph. Write your topic in the middle square. Write reasons that support your opinion in the smaller squares.**

Reason	**Reason**

Topic Sentence

Reason	**Reason**

Revising   Use this checklist to revise.

☐ Do you persuade others to think a certain way?

☐ Do you have good reasons that support your opinion?

☐ Are there facts or details that need to be added?

Editing/Proofreading   Use this checklist to correct mistakes.

☐ Is your paragraph indented?

☐ Is every word or special term spelled correctly?

☐ Does every sentence start with a capital letter?

☐ Does every sentence end with correct punctuation?

Publishing   Use this checklist to prepare for publication.

☐ Write or type a neat copy.

☐ Read your paragraph one more time. Make sure all the parts are there.

Name _____ Date _____

/o͞o/ spelled *u, u_e, _ew, _ue*

Focus

- The /o͞o/ sound sounds like the word *new*.
- Some ways that the /o͞o/ sound can be spelled are *u, u_e, _ew,* and *_ue*.

Practice **Sort the spelling words under the correct heading.**

Word List

1. clue
2. blew
3. lure
4. June
5. student
6. dew
7. grew
8. due
9. ruby
10. overdue

Challenge Words

11. blueberry
12. salute
13. fluid
14. newsroom

/o͞o/ Spelled *u:*

1. _____ 2. _____

/o͞o/ Spelled *u_e:*

3. _____ 4. _____

/o͞o/ Spelled *ew:*

5. _____ 6. _____

7. _____

/o͞o/ Spelled *ue:*

8. _____ 9. _____

10. _____

Apply **Meaning Strategy** Write the spelling word next to its meaning clue.

15. small drops of water found in the morning _____

16. used air to move _____

17. time for something to be finished or turned in _____

18. past the time that something should be finished _____

Visualization Strategy Circle the correct spelling for each spelling word. Write the correct spelling on the line.

19. ruby   rooby   _____

20. clew   clue   _____

21. grew   grue   _____

22. Jewn   June   _____

23. lure   lewr   _____

24. student   stewdunt   _____

Name _____ **Date** _____

Possessive Nouns

- A **noun** is a person, place, or thing.
- A **possessive word** shows ownership.
- A **possessive noun** ends in an apostrophe s ('s).
- A **plural possessive noun** ends in just an apostrophe (').

Example

Singular: *Jennifer's* mother works at the library.

Plural: The *books'* covers were torn.

Practice Write the possessive form of the noun in parentheses ( ) on the blank line.

1. I played with my _____ pet hamster. (friend)

2. The _____ dresses were green. (girls)

3. _____ brother knows a lot of magic tricks. (Megan)

4. My _____ saddle is brand new. (horse)

5. The _____ suggestion was very helpful. (librarian)

Possessive Pronouns

Focus

- A **possessive pronoun** takes the place of a possessive noun. There is no apostrophe (') at the end.

Example

Singular: *Jennifer's* mother works at the library.
   Her mother works at the library.

Plural: The *books'* covers were torn.
   Their covers were torn.

Practice   **Circle the correct *pronoun* to replace the underlined noun.**

1. <u>Andrew</u> found a treasure map buried in the yard. (he, his)

2. We went to <u>Beth's</u> house after school yesterday. (she, her)

3. The <u>peacock's</u> feathers were very colorful. (its, you)

Name _____ Date _____

/oo/ Sound/Spellings

Focus The /**oo**/ sound can be spelled with **oo**. The **oo** spelling pattern is usually found in the middle of a word.

Practice Use the letters in parentheses ( ) to write a word on the blank line with the oo spelling pattern.

1. (b, k) _____

2. (f, t) _____

3. (w, d) _____

4. (h, k) _____

5. (h, d) _____

6. (c, k) _____

7. (s, t, d) _____

8. (s, h, k) _____

Apply Read each word and write a new rhyming word on the blank line.

1. book _____

2. hood _____

3. shook _____

4. look _____

5. stood _____

Complete each sentence by writing one of the above words on the blank line.

1. Our class is reading a _____ about animals and camouflage.

2. I put the _____ on my head when it started to rain.

3. Charlie _____ in line to ride the rollercoaster.

4. You have to _____ closely to see an octopus in hiding.

5. The earthquake _____ the ground.

Name _____ Date _____

Prefix *dis–*

Focus
- A **prefix** is added to the beginning of a word and changes the meaning of that word.
- The prefix **dis–** means "the opposite of", or "not."

Example
  dis– (not) + like = dislike (to not like)

Practice Add the prefix *dis–* to the base words below. Write the new word on the first line. Then write the meaning of the new word.

Base Word	New Word	New Meaning
1. obey	_____	_____
2. agree	_____	_____
3. trust	_____	_____
4. approve	_____	_____

Apply Write a sentence using one of the new words above.

_____

Focus

- A **prefix** is added to the beginning of a word and changes the meaning of that word.
  - The prefix **un–** means "not."

Example

un– (not) + happy = unhappy (not happy)

Practice Add the prefix un– to the base words below. Then write the meaning of the new word.

Base Word	New Word	New Meaning
1. lock	_____	_____
2. ripe	_____	_____
3. fair	_____	_____
4. stuck	_____	_____
5. kind	_____	_____

Apply Fill in the blank with the prefix dis– or un– to create a new word that makes sense in the sentence.

1. Joe used a key to _____lock the door.

2. Mr. Collins does not like _____honesty.

3. It is _____usual for me to _____obey my parents.

4. I was in _____belief that the suitcase was _____latched.

Name _____ Date _____

Selection Vocabulary

Focus

creatures: *n.* Plural of **creature**: a living thing.

delay: *v.* To take place at a later time.

glides: *v.* Moves in a smooth way.

designed: *v.* Past tense of **design**: to plan or make.

fade: *v.* To lose color or brightness.

proceeds: *v.* Moves on or continues.

Practice **Draw a line from each word on the left to its definition on the right.**

1. designed

2. fade

3. creatures

4. proceeds

5. glides

6. delay

a. living things

b. planned or made

c. moves in a smooth way

d. to lose color or brightness

e. to put off

f. moves on or continues

Apply Write the word from the box that matches each
definition below.

creatures	glides	fade
delay	designed	proceed

1. The hooks of a masked crab are _____ to hold
   seaweed to its shell.

2. Many _____ use camouflage to stay safe.

3. An octopus _____ along the ocean floor.

4. Other animals _____ by the sea dragon since it
   looks like seaweed.

5. Stripes on a cuttlefish can _____, leaving it just
   one color.

6. We had to _____ reading *How to Hide an Octopus
   and Other Sea Creatures* until we finished *Animals in Hiding*.

**Draw a picture of a *creature* that is *designed* to *glide*
as it *proceeds* along in the ocean.**

Name _____ Date _____

Writing a Book Report

Think

Audience: Who will read your book report?

_____

Purpose: What is your reason for writing a book report?

_____

Prewriting

Plan your report. Answer each question shown below.

What is the title?

Who is the author?

Who are the main characters?

What happened in the story?
Beginning:

Middle:

Ending:

How do I feel about the book?

Revising   Use this checklist to revise.

- ☐ Did you introduce the title and the author?
- ☐ Do you write about the most important parts?
- ☐ Did you use order words when telling the story events?
- ☐ Did you tell how you feel about the book and why?

Editing/Proofreading   Use this checklist to correct mistakes.

- ☐ Is your paragraph indented?
- ☐ Is every word or special term spelled correctly?
- ☐ Did you capitalize character's names, place names, and book titles?
- ☐ Did you underline the title of the book?
- ☐ Does every sentence start with a capital letter?
- ☐ Does every sentence end with correct punctuation?

Publishing   Use this checklist to prepare for publication.

- ☐ Write or type a neat copy.
- ☐ Have the book or book cover ready to share.

Name _____ **Date** _____

The /oo/ sound

Focus
- The /oo/ sound is spelled *oo* as in the word *cook*.

Practice **Sort the spelling words under the correct heading.**

Word List
1. look
2. good
3. soot
4. shook
5. stood
6. foot
7. brook
8. wood
9. hoof
10. hook

Challenge Words
11. uncooked
12. childhood

Write the spelling words that rhyme with *cook*.

1. _____ 2. _____

3. _____ 4. _____

Write the spelling words that rhyme with *hood*.

5. _____ 6. _____

7. _____

Write the spelling words that rhyme with *woof*.

8. _____

Write the other spelling words with the /oo/ sound.

9. _____ 10. _____

The /oo/ sound

Pronunciation Strategy Choose the correct spelling for each word. Then, pronounce each word carefully and write it on the line below.

1. look   luk   _____

2. fute   foot   _____

3. stuud   stood   _____

4. hufe   hoof   _____

5. shook   shuck   _____

Consonant-Substitution Strategy Replace the underlined letter in each word with a new letter to form a spelling word.

1. cook + h =   _____

2. hood + g =   _____

3. crook + br =   _____

4. foot + s =   _____

5. stood + w =   _____

Name _____ Date _____

Conjunctions and Compound Sentences

Focus

- A **compound sentence** is made when two sentences with similar ideas are combined into one sentence.

- A **conjunction** is a word that connects words or ideas. *And*, *or*, and *but* are conjunctions.

Example

Rosa walked to the mailbox. She mailed the letter.

Rosa walked to the mailbox **and** she mailed the letter.

Practice Put an X next to the sentences that can be combined because they are about the same topic.

1. The dog barked. He wagged his tail. _____

2. Jason ran home. The sun was shining. _____

3. Seth hit the ball. He ran to first base. _____

4. The car was going fast. We were eating lunch. _____

5. Nick went to the phone. He answered it. _____

Apply **Read the sentences. Write a *conjunction (and, or, but)* on the blank line to complete each *compound sentence.***

1. We may skip to school _____ we will not be late.

2. Susie will buy a birthday card _____ she may make a card instead.

3. I am wearing a blue cap _____ I am wearing a blue jacket today.

4. My teacher said it might rain tomorrow _____ we are still going on our class field trip.

5. The cat loves to play with yarn _____ she also plays with a ball.

6. Joe will read a book about cars _____ he may read about dinosaurs.

Use the *conjunction* in parentheses ( ) to write your own *compound sentence.*

1. (and) _____

2. (but) _____

3. (or) _____

Name _____ **Date** _____

/ow/ Sound/Spellings

Focus The **/ow/** sound can be spelled **ow** or **ou_**.

Practice Read the sentence. Change the word in the box to make a new rhyming word to complete the sentence. Write the new word on the blank line.

1. | **brown** | The queen's _____ is made of gold and jewels.

2. | **found** | Worms and other animals live under

   the _____.

3. | **couch** | A baby kangaroo stays in its mother's

   _____.

4. | **town** | I knew Eric wasn't happy when I saw the

   _____ on his face.

5. | **chowder** | Suki likes to use lotion and _____ after her bath.

6. | **round** | The phone makes a funny _____ when it rings.

Apply **Read the sentence. Circle the word that completes each sentence. Write the word on the line.**

1. The baby weighed eight _____ when it was born.

   a. pownds   **b.** pounds   **c.** ponds

2. When our dog gets upset he will start to _____.

   a. growl   **b.** ground   **c.** groul

3. The _____ cheered as our team won the game.

   a. crod   **b.** croud   **c.** crowd

4. Erin spilled milk on her new _____.

   a. blouse   **b.** blows   **c.** blues

Read each hint. Fill in the blank with *ow* or *ou* to complete the word.

1. A small animal that squeaks and likes cheese.   m____se

2. It has petals and a stem.   fl____er

3. You can use one to dry off after swimming.   t____el

4. Something that you can sit on.   c____ch

Name _____ **Date** _____

Prefix *mis–*

Focus

- A **prefix** is added to the beginning of a word and changes the meaning of that word.

- The prefix **mis-** means bad, wrong, or incorrectly.

Example

  mis- (incorrectly) + spell = misspell (to spell wrong or incorrectly)

Practice Add the prefix *mis-* to the base words below. Write the new word on the first line. Then write the new meaning of the new word.

Base Word	New Word	New Meaning
1. count	_____	_____
2. behave	_____	_____
3. match	_____	_____
4. place	_____	_____

Apply Write a sentence using one of the new words above.

1. _____

Prefix *mid-*

- A **prefix** is added to the beginning of a word and changes the meaning of that word.

- The prefix **mid-** means middle.

Example

      mid- (middle) + year = midyear

                                 (in the middle of the year)

Add the prefix *mid-* to the base words below. Write the new word on the first line. Then write the new meaning of the new word.

Base Word	New Word	New Meaning
1. day	_____	_____
2. week	_____	_____
3. night	_____	_____

Fill in the blank with the prefix *mis-* or *mid-* to create a new word that makes sense in the sentence.

1. Did I _____ understand your directions to the game?

2. The employee worked on her _____ year review.

3. We have a _____ morning recess break at school.

4. It is easy to _____ count when you have a lot of items.

Name _____ **Date** _____

Selection Vocabulary

Focus

glossy: *adj.* Bright and shiny.

reeds: *n.* Plural of **reed;** tall grass.

bank: *n.* The land along a stream.

delicate: *adj.* Not strong.

temper: *n.* Mood.

admired: *v.* Past tense of **admire;** to think well of someone or something.

Practice **Write the vocabulary word next to the definition.**

1. not strong _____

2. mood _____

3. bright and shiny _____

4. tall grass _____

5. the land along a stream _____

6. thought well of _____

Apply Write a vocabulary word on the line to complete each sentence.

glossy	bank	temper
reeds	delicate	admired

1. The bird hid in the _____.

2. Julio has a bad _____.

3. The _____ was muddy and wet.

4. My dad _____ the picture.

5. Maria brushed her _____ hair.

6. Her dress was trimmed with _____ lace.

Answer the following questions about "How the Guinea Fowl Got Her Spots."

1. Who has a bad **temper** in the story? _____

2. Who hid in the **reeds**? _____

3. Which character do you **admire**? _____

   Why?_____

4. Which animal would you describe as **delicate**? _____

Name _____ Date _____

Classify and Categorize

- A writer often includes many details in a story. **Classifying** or **Categorizing** the information can show how details are related.

- Readers sort information into different groups or **categories**. This helps them understand and remember what they read.

Classify the following animals by writing the animal name under the category where it belongs.

| polar bear | octopus | guinea fowl | crab spider |
| leaf insect | masked crab | cuttlefish | sea dragon |

Land Animals   **Sea Animals**

_____   _____

_____   _____

_____   _____

_____   _____

Apply **Use the information to classify the animals into the correct category.**

1. **crab spider:** changes color to match flowers

2. **cuttlefish:** stripes can fade, leaving it one color

3. **leaf insect:** stays safe because other animals think it is a leaf

4. **katydid:** looks like a leaf to fool other animals

5. **guinea fowl:** spots help it blend in and hide

6. **sea dragon:** other animals go by thinking it is seaweed

7. **octopus:** changes color and can go from smooth to rough to blend in

8. **sargassum fish:** fools animals by looking like seaweed

Uses mimicry to hide

Uses colors and patterns to hide

_____ _____

_____ _____

_____ _____

_____ _____

Name _____ Date _____

Writing a Folktale

Think **Audience: Who** will read your folktale?

_____

Purpose: What is your reason for writing a folktale?

_____

Prewriting Use the story map to plan your folktale.

Title	
Characters	
Setting	
Problem	
Solution	
Problem	
Solution	
Outcome	
Moral	

Revising Use this checklist to revise.

☐ Does your folktale tell a lesson?

☐ Do you use time and order words?

☐ Does the problem get solved at the end of the story?

Editing/Proofreading Use this checklist to correct mistakes.

☐ Is every word or special term spelled correctly?

☐ Did you capitalize character's names and place names?

☐ Does every sentence start with a capital letter?

☐ Does every sentence end with correct punctuation?

☐ Do your sentences begin in different ways?

Publishing Use this checklist to prepare for publication.

☐ Give your folktale a title. Remember to underline your title.

☐ Write or type a neat copy.

Name _____ **Date** _____

/ow/ spelled *ow, ou_*

Focus
- The /ow/ sound sounds like the word cow or out.
- It can be spelled *ow* and *ou_*.

Word List
1. ouch
2. hour
3. now
4. loud
5. crowd
6. down
7. sound
8. town
9. howl
10. round

Challenge Words
11. birdhouse
12. outside
13. shower

Practice **Sort the spelling words under the correct heading.**

The /ow/ sound spelled *ow*

1. _____ 2. _____

3. _____ 4. _____

5. _____

The /ow/ sound spelled *ou*

6. _____ 7. _____

8. _____ 9. _____

10. _____

/ow/ spelled *ow, ou_*

Apply **Rhyming Strategy** Write the spelling word or words that rhyme with each word below.

1. grouch _____

2. cow _____

3. crown _____ _____

4. found _____ _____

5. fowl _____

Visualization Strategy Circle the correct spelling for the following words. Then write the correctly spelled word on the line.

1. lowd   loud   _____

2. croud   crowd   _____

3. hour   ower   _____

Name _____ Date _____

Synonyms/Antonyms

Focus
- Synonyms are words that have the same, or nearly the same meanings.
- Antonyms are words that are opposite or nearly opposite in meaning.

Practice **Complete the sentences below with a synonym for the given word.**

1. small   The _____ mouse ate cheese.

2. ill   I missed school because I was _____.

3. large   Did you see the _____ elephant at the zoo.

4. leaped   The frog _____ onto the rock.

Complete the sentences below with an antonym for the given word.

1. short   The _____ giraffe was eating leaves off the tree.

2. up   Miguel walked _____ the stairs.

3. full   The milk bottle is _____.

4. found   Sara _____ her mittens.

Write the word from the box that is a synonym.

mad	shake	yell	glad

1. tremble _____

2. happy _____

3. scream _____

4. angry _____

Write the word from the box that is an antonym.

above	worst	narrow	front

1. best _____

2. back _____

3. wide _____

4. below _____

Name _____ Date _____

/o͞o/, /oo/, and /ow/ Spelling/Sound Review

Focus
• The /o͞o/ sound can be spelled using **oo, u, u__e, _ew,** or **_ue.**
• The /oo/ sound is spelled **oo.**
• The /ow/ sound can be spelled **ow** or **ou_.**

Practice **Use the words in the box to complete each sentence.**

| hoop | foot | truth | glued |
| flute | loud | allowed | chew |

1. I _____ the pieces of paper together.

2. Always tell the _____.

3. Eric was not _____ to play in the rain.

4. He threw the basketball into the _____.

5. It is important to _____ your food slowly.

6. Hannah is learning how to play the _____.

7. The _____ noise hurt my ears.

8. Jesse hurt his _____ when he slipped on the ice.

Apply **Circle the correct spelling for each word and then write the word on the line.**

1. knew   nue   _____

2. toob   tube   _____

3. raccoon   racone   _____

4. house   howse   _____

5. dewty   duty   _____

6. stude   stood   _____

7. true   trew   _____

8. arownd   around   _____

9. flower   flouer   _____

10. stood   stoud   _____

Inflectional and Comparative Endings

Focus
- The *inflectional endings* *-ing* and *–ed* can be added to a base word. The meaning of the word is not changed, only the form and function.
- The ending *-ing* lets you know something is happening now.
- The ending *-ed* lets you know something has already happened.
- *Comparative ending -er* shows a comparison between two things.

Practice Add *–ing* and *–ed* to the following words. Write each new word on the line.

1. walk _____ _____

2. work _____ _____

3. help _____ _____

Add *–er* to the following words. Write the new word on the line.

1. fast _____ **2.** young _____

Irregular Plurals

Focus
- **Plural** words show that there is more than one. Adding **–s** or **–es** to a word makes it a regular plural.

- *Irregular Plurals* still mean that there is more than one. Instead of adding an **–s** or **-es**, the entire word is changed to make it plural.

Example
      man   men

- Some words stay the same even when there is more than one.

Example
      deer   deer

Practice **Draw a line to match the singular word to its *irregular plural*.**

1. woman   **a.** people

2. person   **b.** women

3. tooth   **c.** teeth

Circle the correct word to complete each sentence.

1. My (foots   feet) fit perfectly in the new shoes.

2. A large flock of (sheep   sheeps) grazed in the field.

3. The (shelves   shelfes) were covered with dust.

Name _____ Date _____

Selection Vocabulary

Focus

natural: *adj.* Acting on information one is born with.

protective: *adj.* Keeps out of danger or away from harm.

unaware: *adj.* Not watchful or mindful.

coloration: *n.* The way something is colored.

available: *adj.* Being in the area and ready to use.

imitator: *n.* One who copies something or someone.

Practice **Circle the vocabulary word in each sentence. Write the definition on the line.**

1. It is natural for animals to hide for protection.

_____

2. Many animals have coloration that helps them hide.

_____

3. An animal can be an imitator and look like something else.

_____

4. If animals are caught unaware they will still try to hide.

_____

5. Some animals have protective fur that changes color with the seasons.

_____

6. Animals will also use other things that are available to help camouflage.

_____

Apply **Circle *Yes* or *No* if the boldfaced definition for the underlined word makes sense.**

1. A turtle has a <u>protective</u> shell.
keep out of danger .... Yes   No

2. The mouse was <u>unaware</u> of the owl.
acting on information born with .... Yes   No

3. I keep my umbrella <u>available</u> for rainy days.
in the area and ready to use .... Yes   No

4. The <u>coloration</u> of my book makes it hard to see.
one who copies something .... Yes   No

5. It is <u>natural</u> to want to have friends.
acting on information born with .... Yes   No

6. Jenna's sister is an <u>imitator</u>, always acting like her.
one who copies someone .... Yes   No

Name _____ **Date** _____

Types of Camouflage

Look back over the selections you have read. Name some of the animals and tell how they camouflage themselves.

Animal	Camouflage
1.	
2.	
3.	

Which animals use the same kind of camouflage?

_____

Which animals use a different way to camouflage themselves?

_____

Name _____ **Date** _____

Writing a Make-Believe Story

Think

Audience: Who will read your story?

_____

Purpose: What is your reason for writing your story?

_____

Prewriting

Setting (where the story takes place)		**Characters** (people or animals in story)
	Title (name of the story)	
Problem (something causing trouble)		**Solution** (how the problem is fixed)

Revising Use this checklist to revise.

☐ Does your fantasy have a beginning, middle, and end?

☐ Are the events in the right order?

☐ Does the problem get solved at the end of the story?

Editing/Proofreading Use this checklist to correct mistakes.

☐ Is every word or special term spelled correctly?

☐ Did you capitalize character's names and place names?

☐ Does every sentence start with a capital letter?

☐ Does every sentence end with correct punctuation?

☐ Do your sentences begin in different ways?

Publishing Use this checklist to prepare for publication.

☐ Write or type a neat copy.

☐ Include a 'Note from the Author' telling what you like best about this story.

☐ Draw a picture of the characters and setting.

Name _____ Date _____

Review: Lessons 1–4

Focus

- The /o͞o/ sound sounds like the word *moo*. It can be spelled *oo*, *u*, *u_e*, *_ew*, and *_ue*.
- The /oo/ sound sounds like the word *look*. It is spelled *oo*.
- The /ow/ sound sounds like the word *now*. It can be spelled *ow* and *ou_*.

Word List

1. blue
2. rude
3. frown
4. cookie
5. plow
6. count
7. duty
8. cool
9. scout
10. books

Challenge Words

11. looser
12. snowplow

Practice Sort the spelling words under the correct heading.

The /o͞o/ sound

1. _____ 2. _____

3. _____ 4. _____

The /oo/ sound

5. _____ 6. _____

The /ow/ sound

7. _____ 8. _____

9. _____ 10. _____

Review: Lessons 1–4

Apply **Consonant-Substitution Strategy** Replace the underlined letter or letters with the new letter or letters to make a spelling word.

1. <u>c</u>ooks + b = _____

2. <u>tr</u>ue + bl = _____

3. scou<u>r</u> + t = _____

4. <u>d</u>own + fr = _____

5. ru<u>l</u>e + d = _____

Rhyming Strategy Write the spelling word that rhymes with each word below. The spelling word will have the same spelling pattern as the rhyming word.

1. mount _____

2. fool _____

3. rookie _____

4. brow _____

Name _____ Date _____

Colons

Focus
- **Colons** are used to introduce a list. **Commas** should separate the items in the list.
- **Colons** also separate the hour and the minutes when you write the time.

Practice **Write the time written in each sentence using numbers on the blank line after the sentence.**

1. At **two-ten** the doors are locked. _____

2. We must leave the house by **one-thirty**. _____

3. Her birthday party will begin at **five o'clock**. _____

4. **Twelve-fifteen** is our lunchtime. _____

Add missing colons and commas to the following sentences.

1. Place these things in your suitcase shoes shorts and shirts.

2. These are the best things in life love music and friends.

3. Your backpack should have these items paper pencils and folders.

Name _____ **Date** _____

Write colons and commas where they have been left out in the paragraph below.

Ann's alarm woke her up at 7 30. She had to do many things to get ready shower, dress, and brush her teeth. It was 8 00 when she came downstairs to eat. For breakfast she had the usual eggs toast and milk. The bus arrived at 8 15 on the dot. Ann sat on the bus with her three best friends Margaret Tonya and Brittany. Her watch said it was 8 30 when she arrived at school. She was ready to start her day.

Write a sentence using the time or list in parentheses ( ). Write the time in numbers and use colons and commas where needed.

1. (four-twenty) _____

_____

2. (pencils paper erasers) _____

_____

3. (nine-ten) _____

_____

4. (elephants zebras tigers) _____

_____

Name _____ Date _____

/aw/ Sound/Spellings

Focus The /**aw**/ sound can be spelled with **aw** or **au_**.

Practice **Read each sentence. Circle the word that correctly completes the sentence.**

1. Kirsten likes to paint and _____.
   a. drau   **b.** draw   **c.** draue

2. The train _____ us to be late.
   a. caused   **b.** cawse   **c.** caosed

3. The kitten licked its _____.
   a. pah   **b.** paw   **c.** pau

4. What time will they _____ the space shuttle?
   a. lawnch   **b.** luwnch   **c.** launch

5. Will you please help me _____ the firewood?
   a. hall   **b.** hawl   **c.** haul

6. We had a picnic on the _____.
   a. lawn   **b.** laun   **c.** luwn

7. Ms. Wilhem _____ math last year.
   a. taught   **b.** tawght   **c.** tahght

Apply **Write *au* or *aw* in each blank to make a word that completes the sentence.**

1. My favorite flavor of jelly is str_____berry.

2. The marks on the tree were made by a bear's sharp

   cl_____s.

3. E.B. White is the _____thor of the book *Charlotte's Web*.

4. There was too much tomato s_____ce on the pizza.

5. Janelle thought the movie was _____ful.

6. Most babies cr_____l before they learn to walk.

7. A kite was c_____ght in the tree's highest branches.

Write a rhyming word for each word below.

1. lawn _____

2. pause _____

3. jaw _____

4. haul _____

Name _____ Date _____

The Suffixes *-er and -ness*

Focus
- A **suffix** is added to the end of a base word. Adding a suffix changes the meaning of the word.
- The **suffix -ness** means "the state of being."

Example

dark + ness = darkness (the state of being dark)

- The **suffix -er** can mean "*one who.*"

Example

paint + er = painter (one who paints)

Practice Add the suffix *–er* to the base words below and write the new word. Then write the meaning of the new word.

1. speak + er = _____ Meaning: _____

2. teach + er = _____ Meaning: _____

Apply Complete the sentence by adding *–er* to one of the words. Write the word on the blank line.

There is a lot of new work to be done, so we will hire a

_____.

Add the suffix *–ness* to the base words below and write the new word. Then write the meaning of the new word.

1. late + ness = _____ Meaning: _____

2. still + ness = _____ Meaning: _____

Apply Add the *–ness* suffix to a word from the box before writing it on the line.

ill	dark	sad

1. Chickenpox is an example of an _____.

2. It was easy to see John's _____ on his face.

3. My flashlight helped me walk in the _____.

Name _____ Date _____

Selection Vocabulary

Focus

brave: *adj.* Not afraid.

puffing: *v.* Breathing in short breaths.

avalanche: *n.* Stones or snow rolling down a mountain.

trembling: *v.* Shaking.

afraid: *adj.* Feeling fear.

leaping: *v.* Jumping.

Practice Draw a line from the vocabulary word to the correct definition.

1. trembling

2. leaping

3. brave

4. avalanche

5. puffing

6. afraid

a. not afraid

b. stones or snow rolling down a mountain

c. feeling fear

d. jumping

e. shaking

f. breathing in short breaths

Apply **Write a vocabulary word in each blank to complete the sentence.**

Frog and Toad wanted to be _____ together.

They were not _____ as they began their

adventure. Frog was _____ over rocks and

Toad was _____ behind him. A snake left them

_____ with fear. Then the _____

sent them running away. Finally, a hawk caused them to run

home. Frog and Toad stayed at home a long time feeling brave.

Write a sentence for three of the vocabulary words.

1. _____

_____

2. _____

_____

3. _____

_____

Name _____ Date _____

Interview

What questions will you ask in your interview about a brave act? On these pages, write the questions you will use. As you ask each question during the interview, use the space below the question to take notes about the answers.

1. **Question:** _____

   _____

   Answer: _____

   _____

2. **Question:** _____

   _____

   Answer: _____

   _____

3. **Question:** _____

   _____

   Answer: _____

   _____

4. Question: _____

_____

Answer: _____

_____

5. Question: _____

_____

Answer: _____

_____

6. Question: _____

_____

Answer: _____

_____

Name _____ **Date** _____

/aw/ spelled *aw, au_*

Focus
- The /aw/ sound sounds like the word *saw*.
- Two ways it can be spelled are *aw* and *au_*.

Word List
1. hawk
2. sauce
3. thaw
4. draw
5. launch
6. crawl
7. yawn
8. author
9. cause
10. vault

Challenge Words
11. squawk
12. daunting

Practice **Sort the spelling words under the correct heading.**

/aw/ spelled *aw*

1. _____

2. _____

3. _____

4. _____

5. _____

/aw/ spelled *au*

6. _____   9. _____

7. _____   10. _____

8. _____

/aw/ spelled *aw, au_*

Apply **Proofreading Strategy** Read the following story. Circle the misspelled words. Write the correctly spelled words on the line.

Spaghetti with meat salls is not hard to make. First, thau out the meat. Next, dral some water into a large pot. Then, boil the noodles. This will cawz them to become soft. Finally, pour the salls onto the spaghetti. Eat and enjoy!

1. _____   4. _____

2. _____   5. _____

3. _____

Meaning Strategy Use the meaning clue to write the correct spelling word on each line.

1. a large place to store money or other valuables _____

2. to make something take off or start _____

3. a kind of large bird _____

4. to move forward on the hands and knees _____

5. someone who writes a book _____

6. to open the mouth and take a deep breath when sleepy _____

Name _____ Date _____

Capitals and Commas in Letter Greetings/Closings

Focus

- The beginning of a friendly letter is called the *greeting* or *salutation*.

- The first word begins with a **capital**.

- A **comma** is written after the name in the greeting.

Example

   Dear Frog**,**

- The end of a friendly letter is called the *closing*.

- The first word begins with a *capital*.

- A **comma** is written after the closing.

- Your name is written *under* the closing.

Example

   Love**,**

   Toad

Practice Write commas in the list of possible greetings and closings for a friendly letter.

1. Dear Oscar _____

2. Respectfully _____
Oliver

3. Best wishes _____
Nola

4. My dear Nina _____

Name _____ Date _____

Capitals and Commas in Letter Greetings/Closings

Apply Add capital letters and commas where they are needed. Use the following proofreading marks: ^ to insert a comma and ≡ under the letters that need to be a capitalized.

dear   frog

I am glad to have a brave friend like you. You were not afraid to climb the mountain. I tried to be brave when the snake wanted us for lunch, even though I could not stop trembling! The avalanche and the hawk were scary, but lucky for us we got away. I felt brave with you when I was hiding in bed and you were in the closet. You are my best friend!

love

toad

Name _____ Date _____

Poetry (Riddle)

Think **Audience: Who** will read your riddle?

_____

Purpose: What is your reason for writing a riddle?

_____

Prewriting **Plan your riddle. Write down the clues and answer to organize your ideas.**

Answer to riddle:

Clue #1:

Clue #2:

Clue #3:

Poetry (Riddle)

Revising Use this checklist to revise.

☐ Does your poem have clues to answer the riddle?

☐ Are your ideas clear?

☐ Do you create a picture in the reader's mind?

☐ Do you need to add more clues?

☐ Can you change any words to be more descriptive?

Editing/Proofreading Use this checklist to correct mistakes.

☐ Is every word or special term spelled correctly?

☐ Does each line begin with a capital letter?

☐ Is the answer to your riddle written?

Publishing Use this checklist to prepare for publication.

☐ Give your poem a title.

☐ Write or type a neat copy.

Name _____ **Date** _____

/aw/ Sound/Spellings

Focus
- The /**aw**/ sound can be spelled with **augh** and **ough**.

Practice **Write the word from the box that best completes each sentence.**

thought	taught	cough	naughty

1. Brittany _____ the movie started at five o'clock.

2. Our _____ dog chewed the newspaper.

3. Mr. Owens _____ me how to play chess.

4. I have a bad _____ with my cold.

Apply **Use the letters in parentheses to make a word with the spelling pattern.**

1. (t, f) _____

2. (d, e, t, r) _____

Name _____ Date _____

/aw/ Sound/Spellings

Focus
- The /**aw**/ sound can be spelled with **all** and **al**.

Practice Read the word in parentheses. Then read the sentence. Change the word in parentheses to make a new rhyming word. Write the new word on the blank line.

1. (*tall*)   I threw the _____ to Joshua.

2. (*walk*)   There was dust from the _____ on my eraser.

3. (*call*)   Be careful not to _____ into the water.

4. (*stalk*)   William can _____ to his friends on the phone.

Apply Circle the correct spelling for each set of words.

1. walet   wallet

2. almost   allmost

3. halway   hallway

4. walked   wallked

Name _____ Date _____

Suffixes –ly and –y

Focus
- A **suffix** is added to the end of a base word. Adding a suffix changes the meaning of the word.
- The **suffix –ly** means 'in a certain way'.

Example

      slow + ly = slowly (in a slow way)

- The **suffix –y** means 'full of'.

Example

      rain + y = rainy (full of rain)

Practice Add –ly or –y to the following words. Write the new word on the line.

1. nice + ly = _____

2. brave + ly = _____

3. deep + ly = _____

4. leaf + y = _____

5. dirty + y = _____

6. boss + y = _____

Apply Add –ly or –y to the base word in parentheses ( ) to complete the sentence.

1. (*fuss*)   My baby sister gets _____ when she is hungry.

2. (*neat*)   Write your name _____ on the paper.

Name _____ Date _____

The Suffix –ed

Focus
- A **suffix** is added to the end of a base word. Adding a suffix changes the meaning of the word.

- The **suffix –ed** shows something has already happened. It changes the tense of the word from present to past tense.

Example

      play + ed = played (past tense of play)

- When a base word has a short vowel followed by a consonant, the consonant is usually **doubled** before adding –**ed.**

Example

      stop + ed = stopped (past tense of stop)

Practice Add the suffix –**ed** to the following words. Make sure to double the final consonant.

Present Tense   **Past Tense**

1. spot + ed = _____

2. swat + ed = _____

3. kiss + ed = _____

4. nod + ed = _____

Word Structure • *Skills Practice 2*

Name _____ Date _____

Selection Vocabulary

Focus

windmills: *n.* Plural of **windmill;** a machine that uses the power of the wind to turn sails.

trickling: *v.* Flowing drop by drop.

dikes: *n.* Plural of **dike;** a thick wall built to hold back water.

numb: *v.* Having no feeling.

flooded: *v.* Past tense of **flood;** to cover with water.

rumbling: *v.* Making a heavy, deep, rolling sound.

Practice Circle the vocabulary words in the word search.

J	T	K	A	V	B	D	M	O
W	R	U	M	B	L	I	N	G
S	I	I	H	N	U	K	P	I
F	C	N	P	U	G	E	O	T
L	K	K	D	H	L	S	W	R
B	L	N	Z	M	A	U	Q	N
R	I	U	W	Q	I	E	A	C
O	N	M	U	G	H	L	S	X
O	G	B	B	T	I	C	L	I
P	X	H	W	I	T	B	C	S
S	L	Q	E	P	G	N	J	Y
C	F	L	O	O	D	E	D	K

Apply **Answer the following questions.**

1. How does a **windmill** work?

_____

_____

2. Why are **dikes** important?

_____

_____

3. What was **trickling** in the story?

_____

4. What made the **rumbling** sound?

_____

5. Why was Peter's finger **numb**?

_____

_____

Name _____ **Date** _____

Cause and Effect

Focus
- **Cause** and **effect** is when one thing makes another thing happen.
- The **cause** is why something happens.
- The **effect** is what happens.

Practice Read each sentence. Write the *effect* (what happened) and the *cause* (why it happened).

1. Because it was hot, my friends and I went swimming.

   Effect: _____

   _____

   Cause: _____

2. Since we wanted to be helpful, we picked up our toys.

   Effect: _____

   Cause: _____

3. When it was my birthday, we had a party.

   Effect: _____

   Cause: _____

 **Look in *"A Hole in the Dike"* for the effects listed below. Then write the cause for each one.**

1. Effect: Peter got off his bike to see what was wrong.

Cause: _____

_____

2. Effect: All the people thanked Peter. They carried him on their shoulders, shouting, "Make way for the hero of Holland! The brave boy who saved our land!"

Cause: _____

_____

Write a sentence of your own that shows a cause and an effect. Write the effect of your sentence and the cause below.

_____

_____

Effect: _____

Cause: _____

Name _____ **Date** _____

Brave People

Write down a famous hero, like George Washington, and then tell why you think that person is brave or shows bravery.

Famous Hero:

_____

Why is he or she brave?

_____

_____

_____

_____

Write down a community worker, like a fireman, and then tell why you think that person is brave or shows bravery.

Community Worker:

_____

Why is he or she brave?

_____

_____

Write down an everyday person, like your grandmother, and then tell why you think that person is brave or shows bravery.

Everyday Person:

_____

Why is he or she brave?

_____

_____

_____

_____

Name _____ Date _____

/aw/ spelled *augh, ough, all, al*

- The /aw/ sound sounds like the word *taught.*
- Some ways the /aw/ sound can be spelled include *augh, ough, all,* and *al.*

Word List

1. walk
2. overall
3. bought
4. call
5. always
6. sought
7. taught
8. caught
9. halt
10. small

Challenge Words

11. daughter
12. chalk

Practice **Sort the spelling words under the correct heading.**

/aw/ spelled *augh*

1. _____ 2. _____

/aw/ spelled *ough*

3. _____ 4. _____

/aw/ spelled *all*

5. _____ 6. _____

7. _____

/aw/ spelled *al*

8. _____ 9. _____

10. _____

/aw/ spelled *augh, ough, all, al*

Apply **Rhyming Strategy** Write the spelling word or words that rhyme with each word below. The spelling word will have the same spelling pattern for the /aw/ sound as the rhyming word.

11. fought _____ _____

12. ball _____ _____

Consonant-Substitution Strategy Replace the underlined letter or letters with the new consonant to make a spelling word.

13. <u>t</u>alk + w = _____

14. <u>s</u>alt + h = _____

15. <u>c</u>aught + t = _____

Name _____ Date _____

Quotation Marks

Focus

- **Quotation marks** are used right before and right after the words a speaker says.

Example

"Help! There's a hole in the dike," Peter said.

- **Quotation marks** are used around the titles of stories, poems, and book chapters.

Example

I like the story "The Hole in the Dike."

Practice **Add quotation marks around the following titles of stories and poems we have read.**

1. Hungry Little Hare

2. Ants! They are hard workers!

Add quotation marks around the speaker's words in each sentence.

1. The Mad Hatter said,   Digital watches are best.

2. Don't eat so fast! exclaimed Little Red Riding Hood.

Read the sentences below. Add quotation marks where needed.

1. My favorite story is Corduroy by Don Freeman.

2. Ron said, I don't think this is the right house.

3. Will you feed my fish while I'm at camp? asked Jeffrey.

4. The story I See Animals Hiding taught me about camouflage.

5. Anna asked, Have you seen my kitten?

6. I love the poem Ants by Marilyn Singer.

7. We will have recess after our story, said Mrs. Baker.

Find three sentences that use quotation marks in "The Hole in the Dike" and write them below. Make sure to correctly place the quotation marks.

1.

2.

3.

　　　　　　　　　　Grammar • *Skills Practice 2*

Name _____ **Date** _____

Poetry (Acrostic Poem)

Think **Audience: Who** will read your poem?

_____

Purpose: What is your reason for writing a poem?

_____

Prewriting **Plan your poem. Write down ideas or phrases for each letter you are using. Ideas do not have to be complete sentences.**

Write the word you want to use for your poem down this side of the line.	Write the words or phrases you want to form from each letter on the left side.

Revising Use this checklist to revise.

☐ Did you choose an easy word for your poem?

☐ Do the words or phrases you use tell about your topic?

☐ Could you add more interesting or descriptive words? (try using a thesaurus)

Editing/ Proofreading Use this checklist to correct mistakes.

☐ Does each word or phrase start with the correct letter of your topic?

☐ Is every word or special term spelled correctly?

☐ Does each line begin with a capital letter?

Publishing Use this checklist to prepare for publication.

☐ Write or type a neat copy.

☐ Find pictures in magazines or on the computer of your topic.

Name _____ Date _____

ough Sound/Spelling

Focus
- The **ough** spelling pattern has many different sounds.
- Adding the letter *t* to the **ough** pattern makes the /aw/ sound.

Practice **Read the following words.**

cough	through	dough	tough

Write the word with the same vowel sound as *no*.

1. _____

Write the word with the same vowel sound as *blue*.

2. _____

Write the word with the same vowel sound as *saw*.

3. _____

Write the word with the same vowel sound as *puff*.

4. _____

Apply Add the written letter to the *ought* pattern.
Write the new word on the line.

1. s + ought = _____

2. f + ought = _____

3. b + ought = _____

4. br + ought = _____

Circle the correct word to complete each sentence.

1. Marcia (bough, bought) a present for her grandma.

2. Do we have (enough, enought) pizza for everyone?

3. I (though, thought) the homework was due tomorrow.

4. The prince (fought, fough) the dragon and won.

5. Tracy used the (dought, dough) to bake cookies.

6. (Althought, Although) I live close to the school, I still ride the bus.

7. Jasmine (brought, bough) her tent on the camping trip.

8. The pirate (sough, sought) the treasure using a map.

Name _____ Date _____

Suffixes *–less* and *–ful*

Focus
- A **suffix** is added to the end of a base word. Adding a suffix changes the meaning of the word.

- The **suffix *–less*** means "*without.*"

Example

    hope + *less* = hopeless (without hope)

- The **suffix *–ful*** means "*full of.*"

Example

    joy + *ful* = joyful (full of joy)

Practice Add the suffix *–less* and *–ful* to the base words below. Write each new word and then the new meaning of each new word.

Base Word	-less	New Meaning	-ful	New Meaning
1. fear	_____	_____	_____	_____
2. pain	_____	_____	_____	_____
3. care	_____	_____	_____	_____

Name _____ **Date** _____

Prefixes and Suffixes as Syllables

Focus
- Words can be broken down into **syllables.**
- Putting a **prefix** or **suffix** on a word adds syllables to the word.

Practice   **Divide the following words into syllables.**

1. restful   _____

2. flawless   _____

3. mistake   _____

4. illness   _____

5. unworthy   _____

Apply   **Add a base word to the prefix or suffix in parentheses ( ). Divide the new word into syllables.**

1. (mid)   _____   _____

2. (ly)   _____   _____

3. (er)   _____   _____

4. (dis)   _____   _____

Name _____ Date _____

Selection Vocabulary

Focus

kingdom: *n.* A country ruled by a king or queen.
blossom: *v.* To bloom.
emperor: *n.* A ruler.
courage: *n.* The strength to overcome fear.

tended: *v.* Past tense of **tend;** to take care of.
transferred: *v.* Past tense of **transfer;** to move something from one place to another.
sprout: *v.* To begin to grow.

Practice Fill in each blank with a vocabulary word from this lesson.

1. Everyone who lived in the _____ loved flowers.

2. Anything that Ping planted would _____.

3. The _____ was looking for someone to take the throne.

4. Despite being _____ to better soil the seed would not grow.

5. No matter what Ping did, the seed refused to _____.

6. Ping _____ to his seed in the empty pot.

7. Only Ping had the _____ to tell the truth.

Apply Tell whether the boldfaced definition that is given for the underlined word in each sentence below makes sense. Circle Yes or No.

1. The <u>emperor</u> is powerful.
   a ruler   Yes   No

2. Sam <u>transferred</u> the book to the library.
   answered   Yes   No

3. The flowers <u>blossom</u> in May.
   to bloom   Yes   No

4. The lion wanted some <u>courage</u>.
   the strength to overcome fear   Yes   No

5. The tulips began to <u>sprout</u>.
   to bloom   Yes   No

6. Everyone in the <u>kingdom</u> liked the queen.
   a country ruled by a king or queen   Yes   No

7. Amy <u>tended</u> to her garden every day.
   want very much   Yes   No

Name _____ Date _____

Poetry (Rhyming Poem)

Think   **Audience: Who** will read your poem?

_____

Purpose: What is your reason for writing a poem?

_____

Prewriting   **Use this graphic organizer to write your topic and details.**

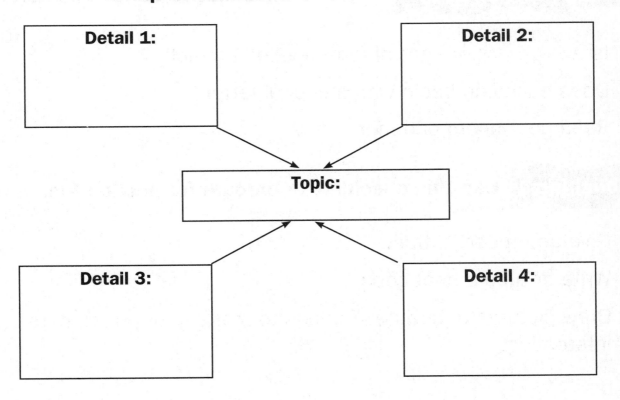

Rhyme is the repeating of the same sounds in two or more words. Circle words from your details and write a rhyming word by that box.

Revising   Use this checklist to revise.

☐ Did you use an interesting idea for your poem?

☐ Does your poem contain information about your topic?

☐ Are your ideas clear?

☐ Are there other words you could use to give more detail about your topic?

☐ Did you use rhyme, repetition, and rhythm?

Editing/Proofreading   Use this checklist to correct mistakes.

☐ Is every word or special term spelled correctly?

☐ Does each line begin with a capital letter?

☐ Read your poem one more time.

Publishing   Use this checklist to prepare for publication.

☐ Give your poem a title.

☐ Write or type a neat copy.

☐ Draw pictures or add decorations to make your poem more interesting.

Name _____ Date_____

Contrast Sound/Spellings for *ough*

Focus
- The spelling patterns *augh* and *ough* can make different sounds.
- The *ough* spelling pattern can sound like /aw/, /ō/, and /u/.

Word List
1. cough
2. dough
3. fought
4. though
5. thought
6. rough
7. although
8. tough
9. ought

Challenge Words
10. thoughtful
11. thorough
12. sourdough

Practice Sort the spelling words under the correct heading.

***ough* with the /aw/ sound**

1. _____

2. _____

3. _____

4. _____

***ough* with the /ō/ sound**

5. _____

6. _____

7. _____

***ough* with the /u/ sound**

8. _____

9. _____

Apply **Rhyming Strategy** Find the spelling word or words that rhyme with each word below.

1. bought _____ _____

2. enough _____ _____

Visualization Strategy Circle the correct spelling for each word below. Then write the correct spelling on the line.

1. coff   cough   _____

2. ought   aut   _____

3. though   thoe   _____

4. dogh   dough   _____

5. although   alltho   _____

Name _____ Date _____

Commas in Dialogue

Focus

- **Quotation marks** are used right before and right after the words a speaker says.

- A **comma** is used to separate the quotation from the person who said it.
Example
  Donna said, "I like dinosaurs!"

- A **comma** is used before the quotation marks that begin a speaker's exact words.
Example
  I said to my dog, "Jump over this log."

- A **comma** is used after the word before the end quotes.
Example
  "I want to watch him jump," said my friend Mai.

Practice **Read the sentences. Put commas where they belong.**

1. Joe said "I need to buy some carrots."

2. Charlotte sighed "Tomorrow is another day."

3. "I cannot sell my cat " I said.

4. "Recess will be in five minutes " my teacher said.

Apply   **Write a comma where it is needed in each sentence.**

1. Misha said "I don't think this is a treasure map."

2. Sasha replied "Oh, yes it is."

3. Misha said "Maybe we'll find gold!"

Draw a line to match the character to the quote.

Emperor   "You did your best, and your best is good
                     enough to present to the Emperor."

Ping's Father   "So today I had to bring an empty pot without a
                     flower. It was the best I could do."

Ping   "Whoever can show me their best in a year's
                     time, will succeed me to the throne."

**Choose one quote and rewrite it using correct quotation marks
and commas.**

Name _____ Date _____

/oi/ Sound/Spellings

Focus • /oi/ can be spelled with **oi** and **_oy**.

Practice Write a letter on the blank line to create a word with the _oy spelling pattern. Write the whole word on the line.

1. _____ oy   _____

2. _____ oy   _____

3. _____ oy   _____

Write a letter on the blank line to create a word with the *oi* spelling pattern. Write the whole word on the line.

1. _____oi_____   _____

2. _____oi_____   _____

3. _____oi_____   _____

4. _____oi_____   _____

Apply Write *oi* or *oy* on the blank line to complete each word with the correct spelling pattern.

1. I need to b_____l the water before I put the pasta in the pot.

2. Is the new baby a girl or a b_____?

3. My little sister pulls my hair just to ann_____ me.

4. Can you p_____nt us in the right direction?

5. Mia likes to hike, and she also enj_____s sailing.

6. Cinderella was able to attend the r_____al ball.

7. Luke added a new quarter to his c_____n collection.

8. Actors in a play speak in loud v_____ces.

9. Tr_____ is my very best friend.

10. I hope the ants and bees won't sp_____l our picnic.

Name _____ **Date** _____

Homographs

Focus
• **Homographs** are words that are spelled and pronounced the same but have different meanings.

Example

bark   Meaning #1: The sound a dog makes.
       Meaning #2: The outer coating of a tree.

Practice   **Use the homographs below to complete the sentences. Use each word twice.**

fan	duck	sink

1. Jonathan is a huge sports _____. The
_____ made a nice breeze to cool us off.

2. Our raft will _____ if anything else is put on it.
It is important to wash your hands in the _____
before eating.

3. We threw crackers to the _____. Todd shouted,
"_____!" when the ball came toward me.

Apply   **Read the two meanings for a homograph. Write the homograph on the blank line.**

1. a vacation or to fall over something _____

2. an insect or to move in the air _____

Name _____ **Date** _____

Homophones

- **Homophones** are words that are pronounced the same but spelled differently and have different meanings.

Example

I can <u>see</u> a fish swimming in the <u>sea</u>.

Practice Use these homophones to complete the sentences.

sun	red	blew
son	read	blue

1. The wind _____ the kite. There was not a cloud in the clear, _____ sky.

2. Our class _____ chapter books this week. Dalmatians rode on the _____ fire truck.

3. The huge, yellow _____ rose in the morning sky. A boy child is the _____ of his parents.

Apply Read the two meanings for a pair of homophones. Write the two homophones on the blank lines.

1. the number after seven   _____

   past tense of eat   _____

Name _____ **Date** _____

Selection Vocabulary

Focus

rugged *adj.* Rough and uneven.

rumble *n.* A heavy, deep, rolling sound.

snapped *v.* Past tense of **snap:** to move quickly and sharply.

squinted *v.* Past tense of **squint:** to look with the eyes partially closed.

shifted *v.* Past tense of **shift:** to change position.

burrowed *v.* Past tense of **burrow:** to dig.

snowdrift *n.* Snow piled up by the wind.

Practice **Write the definition for each vocabulary word.**

1. rugged:

2. squinted:

3. shifted:

4. burrowed:

5. snapped:

6. rumble:

7. snowdrift:

Apply Write the vocabulary word that belongs in the sentence on the blank line.

1. The Iditarod Race has a very _____ trail.

2. Akiak jumped, pulled, and _____ trying to break free.

3. To wait out the storm Akiak _____ in the snow.

4. When the plane _____ the handler let go of the leash.

5. A _____ formed from the blowing snow.

6. Mick _____ looking for a sign.

7. The _____ of the crowd's cheers welcomed the team.

Write three sentences. Use at least one vocabulary word in each sentence.

1.

2.

3.

Name _____ Date _____

Sequence

Focus
- **Sequence** is the order of what happens in a story. Writers often use **time** and **order words** to help readers follow the sequence.
- **Time** words (*winter, today,* and *night*) show the passage of time.
- **Order** words (*first, then, so, when,* and *finally*) show the order in which events happen.

Practice **Read this paragraph carefully. Underline the time and order words.**

Seth gets up every morning at seven o'clock. Every morning he does the same things. He gets dressed first. Then he makes his bed. After that he brushes his teeth. About fifteen minutes later, Seth is ready for breakfast.

Write about something you know how to do, such as making a sandwich. Make sure the sequence of events is clear.

Apply Think about and reread "Akiak." Write down four things that happened in the story. Write them in the order they happened.

1. _____

_____

2. _____

_____

3. _____

_____

4. _____

_____

Draw a picture of each event in the boxes below.

| Event 1 | Event 2 | Event 3 | Event 4 |

Name _____ **Date** _____

News Story

Audience: Who will read your news story?

_____

Purpose: What is your reason for writing a news story?

_____

Prewriting **Use this graphic organizer to write about your topic and its details.**

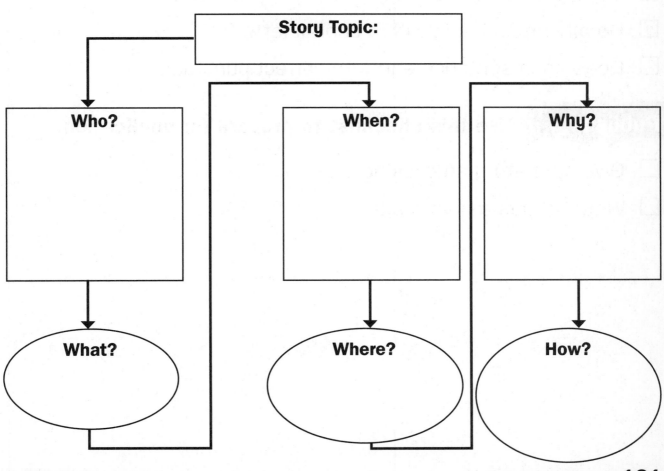

Revising   Use this checklist to revise.

☐ Did you use an interesting idea for your news story?

☐ Does the lead sentence get the reader's attention?

☐ Are your ideas clear and support the topic?

☐ Are the story events written in correct sequence?

☐ Did you use transition words?

Editing/Proofreading   Use this checklist to correct mistakes.

☐ Is every word or special term spelled correctly?

☐ Does each sentence begin with a capital letter?

☐ Do all names begin with a capital letter?

☐ Does each sentence end with correct punctuation?

Publishing   Use this checklist to prepare for publication.

☐ Give your story an exciting title.

☐ Write or type a neat copy.

Name _____ Date _____

/oi/ spelled *oi* and *_oy*

Focus
- The **/oi/** sound sounds like the word *coil.*
- It can be spelled *oi* and *_oy.*

Word List
1. join
2. spoil
3. annoy
4. choice
5. boys
6. voyage
7. coin
8. enjoy
9. boil
10. toy

Challenge Words
11. royal
12. appoint
13. moist

Practice **Sort the spelling words under the correct heading.**

/oi/ spelled *oi*

1. _____

2. _____

3. _____

4. _____

5. _____

/oi/ spelled *oy*

6. _____

7. _____

8. _____

9. _____

10. _____

Apply **Visualization Strategy** Circle the correct spelling for each spelling word. Write the correct spelling on the line.

1. voyage   voij   _____

2. boyal   boil   _____

3. choice   choys   _____

4. anoi   annoy   _____

5. boys   boize   _____

Rhyming Strategy Write the spelling word or words on the line that rhyme with each word below. The spelling word will have the same spelling pattern of the /oi/ sound as the rhyming word.

1. loin _____   _____

2. joy _____

3. foil _____

Name _____ Date _____

Using a Dictionary, a Glossary, and a Thesaurus

Focus
- A **dictionary** is a book that lists words and their definitions.
- A **glossary** is part of a book, usually at the end, that gives definitions for words that appear in that book.
- A **thesaurus** gives synonyms and antonyms for words.

Practice A **Look up the following words in the glossary *of Student Reader, Book 2* and in a dictionary. Write the guide words from each source.**

1. brave

    glossary _____ _____

    dictionary _____ _____

2. puffing

    glossary _____ _____

    dictionary _____ _____

3. rumble

    glossary _____ _____

    dictionary _____ _____

Practice B **Now look the following words up in a thesaurus. Write a synonym and an antonym for each word.**

1. brave

    synonym   _____

    antonym   _____

2. gloomy

    synonym   _____

    antonym   _____

3. stroll

    synonym   _____

    antonym   _____

4. silent

    synonym   _____

    antonym   _____

Name _____ Date _____

Adverbs

- **Adverbs** are words that describe verbs by telling how, where, or when.

Example

We must run **quickly**. (how)

I like to run **outside**. (where)

I **always** run with my friends. (when)

Practice   **Read the sentence. Circle the adverbs.**

1. The Iditarod Race is always run in Alaska.

2. Mushers strictly command their dogs during the race.

3. Injured dogs are easily dropped off at checkpoints.

4. Crowds always cheer for the teams.

5. The dogs work hard to cross the finish line.

Write an adverb to describe each verb.

1. play   (where)

2. talk   (when)

3. move   (how)

Apply **Read the paragraph below. Circle the adverbs.**

Sled dogs have always helped humans. Sled dogs have provided protection, company, and transportation. They are strong and can run swiftly through the snow. These dogs have a desire to pull hard and keep going along the rough land. Mushers can find stopping difficult, even when using the brakes. Sled dogs can easily eat 10,000 calories of food a day. After months of training the team will work together. Once dogs are trained, they can race for many years.

Find three sentences in the story that use adverbs. Write each sentence below and circle the adverb.

1.

2.

3.

Name _____ Date _____

/aw/ and /oi/ Sounds/Spellings

Focus
- /**aw**/ can be spelled *au_, aw, augh, ough, al,* and *all*.
- /**oi**/ can be spelled *oi* and *_oy*.

Practice **Use the words in the box to complete each sentence.**

employer	hallway	audience	adjoining
stalk	thought	lawn	caught

1. Max mows the _____ every Saturday.

2. Performing in front of an _____ can be scary.

3. Our rooms at the hotel were _____.

4. Ava _____ the spelling test was today.

5. The _____ of celery was very crunchy.

6. You can find the bathroom down the _____.

7. My brother _____ the football and scored a touchdown.

8. An _____ pays you money to do a job.

Apply Unscramble the following words and write the new word on the line. Underline the spelling pattern that makes the /aw/ or /oi/ sound in the word.

1. d c a l e l _____

2. d a i v o _____

3. t t a g u h _____

4. e b s e c u a _____

5. l w u a f _____

6. g e u o h n _____

7. t a o m l s _____

8. s e t r o d y _____

Circle the correct spelling for each word.

1. although   althought

2. decoi   decoy

3. threwgh   through

4. choice   choyse

5. cralling   crawling

6. fault   fawlt

7. falling   fawling

Name _____ **Date** _____

Related Words

• Knowing how words are **related** can help readers figure out the meaning of words.

Example

     plant   tree   evergreen   pine

A pine is a type of evergreen. An evergreen is a type of a tree. A tree is a type of a plant.

Practice **Using the example as a guide, write how each group of words is related.**

1. furniture   couch   loveseat

2. story   fairytale   "Cinderella"

Apply **Decide how the words are related. Write a word on the line to complete the group.**

1. animal   bird   _____

2. food   fruit   _____

Name _____ Date _____

Word Families

Focus
- A **base word** is a word that can stand alone. A base word can give a clue to the meaning of other words in the word family.

Example
> **base word:** rain
> **word family:** rainy, raining, rainstorm, rainfall

Practice Write the base word for each word family below.

1. walks, walking, walkway

base word: _____

2. hands, handed, handful

base word: _____

Apply Circle the words in the same word family. Then write the base word the family shares on the blank line.

1. dashed   dusting   dashing

base word: _____

2. ants   anthill   attic

base word: _____

Name _____ **Date** _____

Selection Vocabulary

Focus

mountain lion *n.* A large wild cat that lives in the mountains.

inform *v.* To tell.

dreaded *v.* Past tense of **dread:** to be afraid of or anxious about something.

qualified *v.* Past tense of **qualify:** to be able to do a job or task.

reservation *n.* Land where Native Americans live.

mysterious *adj.* Difficult to understand or explain.

stomping *v.* Walking heavily.

Practice Draw a line matching the vocabulary word with the correct definition.

inform   difficult to understand or explain

dreaded   to be afraid or anxious about

mysterious   walking heavily

stomping   to tell

mountain lion   to be able to do a job or task

qualified   land where Native Americans live

reservation   a wild cat that lives in the mountains

Apply   Circle the correct word that completes each sentence.

1. Spider _____ giving his father the papers from school.

   dreaded   inform   stomping

2. Many Native Americans live on a _____.

   qualified   dreaded   reservation

3. His parents were very proud that he _____ for the spelling bee.

   dreaded   qualified   inform

4. Will was _____ his feet to get the snow off his boots.

   stomping   inform   dreaded

5. The small spider seemed to speak in a _____ way.

   reservation   mysterious   inform

Write one sentence using two of the vocabulary words.

Name _____ Date _____

Author's Purpose

Focus

- Understanding an **author's purpose** helps readers better understand the story. Authors write to *entertain, inform,* and *persuade.*

Rule

- To **inform** is to tell facts about something.

- To **entertain** is to amuse people.

- To **persuade** is to talk people into thinking or doing something.

Example

- China is the largest country.

- The silly puppy fell asleep in the drawer.

- Here is why we should not litter.

Practice   After each sentence, write the purpose.

1. If we all help, we can make our city clean. _____

2. As the sun rose, the ocean sparkled like diamonds. _____

3. This is the oldest fossil known to humans. _____

 **Reread page 267 of "Brave as a Mountain Lion." What is the author's purpose?**

Author's Purpose:

How did the author show purpose:

Write a title to a story as an example for each purpose.

1. entertain:

2. persuade:

3. inform:

Choose one of your titles from above and write the first sentence for that story.

Title: Author's Purpose:

Name _____ Date _____

Play

Think   **Audience: Who** will read your play?

_____

Purpose: What is your reason for writing a play?

_____

Prewriting   **Use this graphic organizer to plan the characters, setting, and plot of your play.**

Characters:

Name:	**Name:**	**Name:**
Age:	**Age:**	**Age:**
Likes:	**Likes:**	**Likes:**
Dislikes:	**Dislikes:**	**Dislikes:**

Setting:

When does the play take place?

Where does the play take place?

What are some sight or sound words to describe the setting?

Plot:

Problem:

Solution:

Revising   Use this checklist to revise.

☐ Does your play have a beginning, middle, and end?

☐ Does the problem get solved?

☐ Are your characters interesting?

☐ Does the dialogue show how characters think and feel?

☐ Will readers be able to follow the events?

☐ Did you use time and order words correctly?

Editing/Proofreading   Use this checklist to correct mistakes.

☐ Is every word or special term spelled correctly?

☐ Does each sentence begin with a capital letter?

☐ Do all names begin with a capital letter?

☐ Does each sentence end with correct punctuation?

☐ Did you use correct grammar with all verbs in the correct tense?

Publishing   Use this checklist to prepare for publication.

☐ Give your play a title.

☐ Write or type a neat copy.

☐ Write character names in **bold** print.

☐ Stage directions should be written in *italics*.

☐ Use regular print for dialogue.

Name _____ Date _____

Review: /aw/ spelled *aw*, *au_*, *augh*, *ough*, *all*, and *al*; /oi/ spelled *oi* and *_oy*

Focus
- The **/aw/** sound can be spelled *aw*, *au_*, *augh*, *ough*, *all*, and *al*.
- The **/oi/** sound can be spelled *oi* and *_oy*.

Practice Sort the spelling words under the correct heading.

The /aw/ sound

1. _____

2. _____

3. _____

4. _____

5. _____

6. _____

The /oi/ sound

7. _____

8. _____

9. _____

10. _____

Word List

1. lawn

2. haul

3. recall

4. stalk

5. thoughts

6. naughty

7. voyage

8. noise

9. loyal

10. rejoice

Challenge Words

11. ointment

12. walnut

13. because

Apply **Visualization Strategy** Look at each word below. If the word is spelled correctly, write the word *correct* on the line. If the word is misspelled, write the correct spelling on the line.

1. stauck _____

2. thoughts _____

3. rejoice _____

4. voiage _____

5. hough _____

Proofreading Strategy Read the story below. Circle any misspelled words. Then write the correctly spelled word on the line.

I can reackal one time I heard a noyze on our front laughn. When I went outside to investigate, I noticed a strange dog tearing through our trash can. Just then, our loil dog Scout chased the notty rascal away. What a sight!

1. _____

2. _____

3. _____

4. _____

5. _____

Name _____ **Date** _____

Verb Tenses

Focus

- Finding the right verb and using the right tense of the verb is important in both speaking and writing.

Rule	Example
• A **present** tense verb tells about something that is happening now.	• I **walk** to school.
• A **past** tense verb tells about something that happened in the past.	• I **walked** to school yesterday.
• A **future** tense verb tells about something that will happen in the future.	• I **will walk** to school tomorrow.

- Some verbs do not add –ed to change from present to past tense. They change in other ways.

Example

     I sing.   I sang.

Practice   **Write the past and future tense for the verb on the blank lines.**

Present Tense	Past Tense	Future Tense
1. look	_____	_____
2. grow	_____	_____
3. drive	_____	_____

Apply Complete each sentence with the correct tense of the boldfaced verb.

1. I **gave** today. Next week I will _____.

2. Yesterday they **fought**. Today they _____.

3. We **are** happy. Last week we _____ happy.

4. Last month I **sang**. Tomorrow I will _____.

5. I can **throw** the ball. Yesterday I _____ the ball.

Write the correct verb tense to replace the underlined verb.

1. I will <u>sang</u> loudly at choir practice. _____

2. Tomorrow Ann will <u>rode</u> with us to school. _____

3. When it snowed, our cat <u>come</u> inside. _____

4. Yesterday, there <u>is</u> nowhere to play. _____

5. Next year I will <u>am</u> in third grade. _____

6. Make sure to <u>looked</u> for cars before crossing the street.

_____

Name _____ **Date** _____

/ow/, /o͞o/, /oo/, /ū/ and /ō/
Sounds and Spellings

Focus
- The **ow** spelling pattern can make the /ō/ sound or the /ow/ sound.
- The **u, u_e, _ue**, and **_ew** spelling patterns can make the /o͞o/ and /ū/ sound.
- The **oo** spelling pattern can make the /o͞o/ and /oo/ sound.

Practice Write the following *ow* spelling pattern words under the correct sound, /ō/ or /ow/.

| crowded | yellow | rookie | booth |
| shallow | eyebrows | groomer | football |

/ow/ | long ō

1. _____   1. _____

2. _____   2. _____

Write the following *oo* spelling pattern words under the correct sound, /o͞o/, or /oo/.

/o͞o/ | /oo/

1. _____   1. _____

2. _____   2. _____

Apply Write each one of the letters in parentheses ( ) on a blank line to make a word with the spelling pattern given. *Letters are not always in order of the blanks. Write the word on the blank line.

1. (r, c) _____ow _____

2. (g, d, l) _____ue_____ _____

3. (h, s, p) _____oo_____ _____

4. (f, r, l, e) _____ow_____ _____

5. (g, r) _____ew _____

6. (t, t, h, r) _____u_____ _____

7. (h, f) _____oo_____ _____

8. (b, s, a) _____u_____e _____

Write a word for each spelling pattern listed below.

1. ow sounding like /ō/ _____

2. ow sounding like /ow/ _____

3. oo sounding like /oo/ _____

4. oo sounding like /ōō/ _____

5. u sounding like /ū/ _____

Name _____ Date _____

Antonyms and Synonyms

- **Synonyms** are words that are similar in meaning. *Happy* and *glad* are synonyms.

- **Antonyms** are words that are opposite in meaning. *Up* and *down* are antonyms.

Practice In each box circle the *synonym* and draw a line under the *antonym* for each word shown.

1. near

close	apart	far

2. winner

helper	loser	champion

3. sick

fell	healthy	ill

Apply Write the synonym or antonym for the word in parentheses that will complete the sentence.

1. (early) If we don't hurry, we'll be _____ for the movie.

2. (bend) There is a _____ in the road up ahead.

3. (float) The rock will _____ when thrown in the water.

Compound Words and Contractions

Focus
- **Compound words** are made when two words are put together to make a new word.
- A **contraction** is a shortened form of a pair of words. An apostrophe (') is used to show where a letter or letters have been removed.

Practice Underline the compound words and circle the contractions in each sentence.

1. Didn't you catch a grasshopper in the yard?

2. Aunt Jenny can't go to the baseball game.

3. Where's the toothbrush my dentist gave me?

Apply Write the two words that make each contraction you circled. Write the two words that make each compound word you underlined.

Contractions

1. didn't _____ _____

2. can't _____ _____

3. where's _____ _____

Compound Words

1. grasshopper _____ _____

2. baseball _____ _____

3. toothbrush _____ _____

Word Structure • *Skills Practice 2*

Name _____ Date _____

Selection Vocabulary

Focus

orchid *n.* A type of flower.

discovered *v.* Past tense of **discover:** to be the first to find, learn of, or observe.

sesame *n.* A tropical Asian plant bearing small, flat seeds used as food and as a source of oil.

chores *n.* Plural of **chore:** a small job around the house.

explorer *n.* A person who travels to a new place for the purpose of discovery.

popular *adj.* Liked or accepted by many people.

wiser *adj.* Smarter.

Practice Draw a line matching the vocabulary word with the correct definition.

1. explorer   **a.** to be the first to find, learn of, or observe

2. wiser   **b.** smarter

3. discovered   **c.** plant bearing small, flat seeds used as food or oil

4. chores   **d.** a type of flower

5. orchid   **e.** a person who travels to a new place for discovery

6. popular   **f.** a small job around the house

7. sesame   **g.** liked or accepted by people

Apply Write a vocabulary word on the blank line to complete each sentence.

orchid	explorer	chores	wiser
sesame	discovered	popular	

1. My family shares the _____ for our house.

2. The music playing on the radio is very _____.

3. I saw an _____ in bloom.

4. Joshua _____ the present hidden in his closet.

5. Is it _____ to read a book or watch television?

6. A _____ plant has many uses.

7. The _____ used a boat for his trip.

Write three sentences using at least one vocabulary word in each sentence.

1. _____

2. _____

3. _____

Selection Vocabulary • *Skills Practice 2*

Name _____ Date _____

Fact and Opinion

- To make stories more interesting, facts and opinions are used.

• A **fact** is something that can be proven true.

Example
The Statue of Liberty is in New York.

• An **opinion** is what someone thinks or feels.

Example
I think the Statue of Liberty is beautiful.

Practice **Look back at "April and Her Family." Copy a sentence that gives facts. Copy a sentence that gives opinions.**

Fact

1. _____

_____

Opinion

1. _____

_____

UNIT 6 Lesson 1

 **Apply** — **Read this paragraph. Draw a line under each sentence that tells a fact. Circle the sentences that give opinions.**

The Statue of Liberty stands in New York Harbor. It was a gift to the United States from France. "Liberty Enlightening the World" is the official name of the statue. Everyone would like to see this famous lady. She is very beautiful. Workers built the statue in France, took it apart, and sent it to America to be reassembled. Maybe they should have made the statue in America. It took twenty-one years to finally complete the statue. Many immigrants have seen this famous lady when they arrived in America. It is the best landmark of the United States. The Statue of Liberty is a symbol of friendship, freedom, and democracy.

Write several sentences about a place you have visited or lived. Make sure you include facts and opinions. After writing, draw a line under each sentence that tells a fact. Circle the sentences that give opinions.

_____

_____

_____

_____

_____

_____

Name _____ Date _____

Personal Letter

Think **Audience: Who** will read your letter?

_____

Purpose: What is your reason for writing a letter?

_____

Prewriting Use this graphic organizer to plan the body of your letter.

1. Start with the date and the word "Dear," then add the person's name.	
2. Explain the topic of your letter.	
3. Tell details about the topic.	
4. Choose a personal closing. It could be "Love," or "Your friend".	

Revising   Use this checklist to revise.

- ☐ Is the topic of your letter clear?

- ☐ Did you leave out anything that you want to put in your letter?

- ☐ Did you include why you went on the visit and describe the place?

- ☐ Did you tell about the things you did at this place?

- ☐ Does your letter sound personal and friendly?

Editing/Proofreading   Use this checklist to correct mistakes.

- ☐ Does each sentence add a new thought to your letter?

- ☐ Is every word or special term spelled correctly?

- ☐ Does each sentence begin with a capital letter and end with correct punctuation?

- ☐ Do all names begin with a capital letter?

- ☐ Could other words be used to give more detail?

Publishing   Use this checklist to prepare for publication.

- ☐ Read your letter one more time. Make sure all of the parts of the letter are there.

- ☐ Write or type your letter.

- ☐ Sign your letter.

- ☐ Address an envelope to mail your letter.

Name _____ **Date** _____

Contrast Sound/Spellings for /ō/ and /ow/, /ōō/ and /ū/, /ōō/ and /oo/

Focus

- The /ō/ sound and the /ow/ sound can both be spelled *ow*.
- The /ōō/ sound sounds like the word *cool*, while the /ū/ sound sounds like the word *cute*.
- The /ōō/ and /oo/ sounds can both be spelled *oo*.

Word List

1. flow
2. flower
3. cook
4. cube
5. tool
6. took
7. nook
8. noon
9. fume
10. loom

Challenge Words

11. moonbeam
12. mountain
13. mowing

Practice Sort the spelling words under the correct heading.

The /ō/ sound spelled *ow*

1. _____

The /ow/ sound spelled *ow*

2. _____

The /ōō/ sound

3. _____

4. _____

5. _____

The /ū/ sound

6. _____

7. _____

The /oo/ sound

8. _____

9. _____

10. _____

Apply **Rhyming Strategy** Find the spelling word or words that rhyme with the following words. The spelling word will have the same sound and spelling pattern as the rhyming word.

11. spoon   _____

12. power   _____

13. fool   _____

14. grow   _____

15. room   _____

16. look   _____ _____ _____

Visualization Strategy Read each word below. If the word is spelled correctly, write the word *correct* on the line. If the word is misspelled, write the correctly spelled word on the line.

17. fyoom   _____

18. cube   _____

Name _____ Date _____

Noun, Verb, Subject, and Predicate Review

Focus

- **Common nouns** name a person, place, thing, or idea. Common nouns do not begin with a capital letter.

- **Proper nouns** name a certain person, place, or thing. Proper nouns begin with a capital letter.

- An **action verb** tells what someone is doing.

- **Linking verbs** connect the parts of a sentence to make it complete.

- A **helping verb** helps the main verb tell something that has happened, is happening, or will happen.

- The **subject** tells what or whom the sentence is about. The **predicate** tells something about the subject.

Practice   Read the following nouns. Write the noun under the correct column. If it is a proper noun make sure to begin with a capital letter.

dancer	dr. green	color	america

Common Nouns   **Proper Nouns**

1. _____   1. _____

2. _____   2. _____

**Read each sentence below. Circle the subject.
Underline the predicate.**

1. Samantha threw the ball.

2. The audience cheered loudly.

3. Judy exercises every day.

4. My teacher read a picture book.

Apply   **Read each sentence. Read the description of a noun
or verb written in parentheses ( ). Write a noun or verb
on the line to complete the sentence.**

1. _____ (proper noun) _____
(action verb) me how to play the piano.

2. My _____ (common noun) _____
(helping verb) swimming like a fish today.

3. That _____ (common noun) _____
(linking verb) my favorite.

**Write three sentences. Circle the subject and underline the
predicate.**

1. _____

2. _____

3. _____

Name _____ Date _____

Silent Consonants

Focus
- **Silent consonants** in a word are not heard when the word is read.

Practice Read each word, and circle the letter that is silent.

1. hour

2. doubt

3. rhyming

4. scene

5. knit

6. wrench

7. lamb

8. island

9. scent

10. listen

11. crumb

12. school

Apply   Circle the correct word to complete each sentence.

1. William ate (haf, half) of the pizza.

2. I did not know the (answer, anser) to her question.

3. The (sente, scent) of baking cookies filled the air.

4. Did you (listen, lisen) to the story?

5. Carol hit her (thum, thumb) with the hammer.

6. There is a stop (sine, sign) in front of my house.

Look at each pair of words with a silent letter spelling pattern. Underline the spelling pattern in each word. Write a third word with the same spelling pattern on the blank line.

1. knee   knot   _____

2. climb   comb   _____

3. wrong   wreck   _____

4. gnat   sign   _____

5. rhombus   rhythm   _____

Name _____ **Date** _____

Prefixes: *dis-*, *un-*, *mis-*, and *mid-*

Focus
- A **prefix** is added to the beginning of a word and changes the meaning of that word.
- The prefix **dis-** means to do the opposite of, or 'not to'
- The prefix **un-** means the opposite of or 'not'
- The prefix **mis-** means bad, wrong, or incorrectly
- The prefix **mid-** means middle

Practice Choose a prefix from above to add to each base word that will make sense. Write the meaning of the new word.

1. _____ month _____

2. _____ agreed _____

3. _____ treat _____

4. _____ planned _____

5. _____ loyal _____

6. _____ adjust _____

7. _____ life _____

8. _____ zipped _____

Apply Choose one of the following prefixes to add to the base word in parentheses ( ) that will complete the sentence. Write the new word on the blank line. Write the meaning of the new word.

dis-	un-	mid-	mis-

1. Karl was _____ (able) to attend the party.

   New Meaning: _____

2. Our seats were in the _____ (section) of the stadium.

   New Meaning: _____

3. My little sister sometimes _____ (obeys) our parents.

   New Meaning: _____

4. I _____ (typed) my book report on the computer.

   New Meaning: _____

5. Joan _____ (wrapped) her present.

   New Meaning: _____

Name _____ Date _____

Selection Vocabulary

Focus

recycling *v.* Using throwaway items for another purpose.

brisk *adj.* Quick and lively.

adopted *v.* Past tense of **adopt:** to take as one's own.

fabric *n.* Cloth.

doe *n.* A female deer.

leather *n.* Material made from animal skin.

citizens *n.* Plural of **citizen:** a person who was born in a country or who chooses to live in and become a member of a country.

shed *n.* A small building used for storing things.

Practice   **Write the vocabulary word for each definition.**

1. cloth   _____

2. to take as one's own   _____

3. a female deer   _____

4. using throwaway items for
another purpose   _____

5. material made from animal skin   _____

6. quick and lively   _____

7. small building used for storing
things

Apply Tell whether the boldfaced definition that is given for the underlined word in each sentence below makes sense. Circle Yes or No.

1. A <u>citizen</u> is allowed to vote.
a member of a country .... Yes   No

2. Miguel <u>adopted</u> the stray kitten.
looked for .... Yes   No

3. The <u>doe</u> ran across the meadow.
a female deer .... Yes   No

4. My coat is made from red <u>fabric</u>.
a small building used for storing things .... Yes   No

5. Doug has <u>leather</u> shoes.
material made from animal skin .... Yes   No

6. Please put the lawn mower back in the <u>shed</u>.
a medium-sized boat .... Yes   No

7. We took a <u>brisk</u> walk.
quick and lively .... Yes   No

8. Our class is learning about <u>recycling</u>.
cloth .... Yes   No

Name _____ Date _____

Cause and Effect

Focus
- When you read, the more you know about what caused something to happen the better you will understand what you read.
- The **cause** is why something happens.
- The **effect** is what happens.

Practice **Read the cause of the following parts of a sentence. Write an effect to complete the sentence.**

1. Because we are friends, _____

_____

2. Since Joe was late, _____

_____

3. When it is the first day of school, _____

_____

4. On a cold day, _____

_____

Read the page from "New Hope." Then write the cause of the given effect.

1. Page 321

Effect: Lars sailed with his family to this country from Denmark.

Cause: _____

2. Page 322

Effect: Lars bought a wagon, two horses, a hunting rifle, tools, a tent, several bags of seeds, and plenty of food in Minnesota.

Cause: _____

3. Page 323

Effect: Peter and Mathilde adopted a dog.

Cause: _____

4. Page 327

Effect: Franz opened a forge.

Cause: _____

5. Page 328

Effect: Lars opened a general store.

Cause: _____

Name _____ **Date** _____

Inquiry

Create a list of "ordinary" and "extraordinary" people. Write one or two things you would like to learn about each person.

"Ordinary" People

1. Name: _____

    a. Question: _____

    _____

    b. Question: _____

    _____

2. Name: _____

    a. Question: _____

    _____

    b. Question: _____

    _____

3. Name: _____

    a. Question: _____

    _____

"Extraordinary" People

1. Name: _____

   a. Question: _____

   _____

   b. Question: _____

   _____

2. Name: _____

   a. Question: _____

   _____

   b. Question: _____

   _____

3. Name: _____

   a. Question: _____

   _____

   b. Question: _____

   _____

Name _____ Date _____

Personal Letter

Think **Audience: Who** will read your letter?

_____

Purpose: What is your reason for writing a letter?

_____

Prewriting Use this graphic organizer to plan the body of your letter.

1. Start the word "Dear," then add the person's name.	
2. Explain the topic of your letter.	
3. Tell details about the topic.	
4. Choose a personal closing. It could be "Love," or "Your friend".	

Revising **Use this checklist to revise.**

☐ Is the reason for writing your letter clear?

☐ Did you leave out anything that you want to put in your letter?

☐ Did you include your feelings for the person?

☐ Did you wish them to get well?

☐ Does your letter sound personal and friendly?

Editing/Proofreading **Use this checklist to correct mistakes.**

☐ Does each sentence add a new thought to your letter?

☐ Is every word or special term spelled correctly?

☐ Does each sentence begin with a capital letter and end with correct punctuation?

☐ Do all names begin with a capital letter?

☐ Could other words be used to give more detail?

Publishing **Use this checklist to prepare for publication.**

☐ Read your letter one more time. Make sure all of the parts of the letter are there.

☐ Write or type your letter.

☐ Sign your letter.

Name _____ Date _____

Silent Letters

Focus
- Silent letters are letters in a word that are not heard when the word is pronounced.

Examples
thumb   should

Word List
1. listen
2. castle
3. rustle
4. whistle
5. rhino
6. answer
7. doubt
8. island
9. would
10. could

Challenge Words
11. chaos

Practice **Sort the spelling words under the correct heading.**

Silent *t*

1. _____

2. _____

3. _____

4. _____

Silent *h*

5. _____

6. _____

Silent *w*

7. _____

Silent *b*

8. _____

Silent *s*

9. _____

Silent *l*

10. _____

11. _____

Silent Letters

Apply **Visualization Strategy** Read each word below. If the word is spelled correctly, write correct on the line. If the word is misspelled, write the correctly spelled word on the line. Then, underline the silent letter or letters in the word.

12. wislle _____

13. island _____

14. could _____

15. rino _____

16. rustle _____

17. dowt _____

18. casul _____

19. listen _____

20. ancer _____

21. would _____

Name _____ Date _____

Using an Encyclopedia

One of the most helpful resources you can use when doing an investigation is an encyclopedia. An **encyclopedia** is a set of books with information on many topics, arranged in alphabetical order. Each book in the set is called a **volume**.

Here is an illustration of an encyclopedia. It has 20 volumes. Count the volumes.

• Use the illustration above to answer the questions below. Information about a person is arranged by the first letter of the person's last name. Write the volume letter or letters where you might find information about the following subjects.

1. Information about Denmark _____

2. Information about the history of blacksmithing _____

3. An entry on Laura Ingalls Wilder _____

4. Information about New York _____

5. An entry on Henri Sorensen _____

6. Information about ferries _____

7. Information about horses _____

• Below are questions that can be answered by looking in an encyclopedia. For each question, write one or more entries, or subjects, under which you would look to find the information. For example, to answer the question, "What is the difference between a dog and a wolf?" you might look under "dog," "wolf," or "animals."

1. What kind of animal is a kangaroo? _____

_____

2. What is the difference between a parrot and

a parakeet? _____

_____

3. Which city has more people living in it, New York

or Los Angeles? _____

_____

4. Who invented baseball? _____

Name _____ Date _____

Capitalization and End Marks Review

Focus
- Every sentence must begin with a capital letter and end with a period, a question mark, or an exclamation point.

Practice **Underline three times (≡) the letters that should be a capital in the paragraph. Add correct end marks that are missing.**

do you know where your ancestors are from your

ancestors are the members of your family that came

before you most people have ancestors who came

to America from another country is your family from

one country or many countries freedom, money, and

safety are examples of some reasons people moved

to America would you be afraid to move to a distant

country our ancestors were very brave people

Apply **Write a sentence about your ancestors. Make sure to use correct capital letters and punctuation.**

1. _____

_____

Complete/Incomplete Sentences and Kinds of Sentences Review

Focus
- A **complete sentence** has a subject and a predicate. In an **incomplete sentence**, or **fragment**, something is missing.

- A **declarative** sentence makes a statement. An **imperative** sentence gives directions or a command. An **exclamatory** sentence shows strong feelings.

Practice Identify the sentences below by writing F for a fragment or R for a run-on sentence. Then write the sentence correctly.

1. the frog lily pad. _____

_____

2. my friend lives in Alabama she will visit me this summer _____

_____

Insert the correct end mark to each sentence. Decide what type of sentence it is and write D for statement, Q for question, I for directions/commands, or E for exclamatory sentences on the line.

1. Don't rock the boat _____

2. Where is your life jacket _____

Name _____ Date _____

Three-letter blends

Focus
- **str   scr   spl   spr**
- The sounds of these letters often combine at the beginning of words. We say the three sounds quickly without any space between them.

Practice Add the blends to the letters on the right to create a word. Write the word on the line. Read the word aloud.

1. *str*   and   _____

2. *scr*   ape   _____

3. *spl*   at   _____

4. *spr*   out   _____

5. *str*   ain   _____

6. *scr*   eam   _____

7. *spl*   otch _____

8. *spr*   ead   _____

Change the beginning blend of two words above to make a new word. Write the word from the list and the new word.

1. _____   _____

2. _____   _____

Apply Choose one of the three letter blends to complete each word. Write the blend on the line in front of the letters. Write the word on the blank line.

str	scr	spl	spr

1. _____ inkled _____

2. _____ ash _____

3. _____ een _____

4. _____ ipe _____

5. _____ urge _____

6. _____ awberry _____

7. _____ int _____

8. _____ ub _____

Write a sentence using a word with the three letter blend written in parentheses ( ).

1. (str) _____

2. (scr) _____

3. (spl) _____

4. (spr) _____

Name _____ Date _____

Inflectional and Comparative Endings

Focus
- The *inflectional endings –ing* **and** *–ed* can be added to a base word. The meaning of the word is not changed, only the form and function. *–ing* lets you know something is happening now. *–ed* is used when something has already happened.

- *Comparative endings* show a comparison between two things. The ending *–er* is usually added to a base word.

Practice **Write each base word under the correct ending. Write the word and add the correct suffix. Write the same base word with each of the inflectional endings. Remember that the** *–er* **ending should be used as a** *comparison.*

young	fail	glow	cheap
moist	earn	high	pick

Inflectional Endings   **Comparative Ending**

  –ing   –ed   –er

1. _____ _____   1. _____

2. _____ _____   2. _____

3. _____ _____   3. _____

4. _____ _____   4. _____

Suffixes –*er* and –*ness*

Focus
- The **suffix –*er*** means "one who."
- The **suffix –*ness*** means "*state of being.*"

Practice Add the suffix to the base word and write the new word. Write the meaning of the new word.

1. surf + er = _____

New Meaning: _____

2. blind + ness = _____

New Meaning: _____

Apply Choose one of the words below and add –er or –ness and write it on the line.

train	light	fond

1. The tiger _____ shouted his commands.

2. Lavender is a _____ shade of purple.

3. Carol has a _____ for puppies.

Name _____ Date _____

Selection Vocabulary

Focus

demanding *v.* Asking for forcefully.

arrested *v.* Past tense of **arrest:** to hold by authority of law.

fair *adj.* Not favoring one more than another.

section *n.* A part.

laws *n.* Plural of **law:** a rule made by a government.

content *n.* What is in something.

graduated *v.* Past tense of **graduate:** to finish school.

prejudice *n.* Unfair treatment of a group of people.

Practice **Fill in each blank with a vocabulary word from this lesson to complete each sentence.**

1. Martin Luther King, Jr. _____ from high school two years early.

2. There was once a "White Only" _____ on public buses.

3. Some _____ kept African Americans out of many schools and jobs.

4. Rosa Parks was _____ for not giving a white man her seat on the bus.

5. Protests were led _____ fair laws for all people.

Apply Use the vocabulary words to complete the following activities.

1. Write about a time that you were not treated in a *fair* way.

_____

_____

2. How did some *laws* affect African American people?

_____

_____

3. Explain how the Montgomery Public Buses were once *prejudiced*.

_____

_____

4. Why was Rosa Parks *arrested*?

_____

_____

5. What was one way Martin Luther King, Jr. *demanded* equal rights for all people?

_____

_____

Name _____ Date _____

Formal Letter

Think **Audience: Who** will read your letter?

_____

Purpose: What is your reason for writing a letter?

_____

Prewriting Use this graphic organizer to plan the body of your letter.

1. **Heading: Start with your name and address.**	
2. **Inside Address: Add the name and address of the person to whom you are writing.**	
3. **Greeting: Start with words "To Whom it May Concern" or "Dear," then add the person's name.**	
4. **Body: Ask for something or share your ideas.**	
5. **Closing: End your letter with "Yours truly" or "Sincerely" and sign your name.**	

Revising Use this checklist to revise.

☐ Is the reason for writing your letter clear?

☐ Do you have enough detail about what you want to say?

☐ Did you stay on the topic?

☐ Are there sentences you can delete?

☐ Is your letter polite?

Editing/Proofreading Use this checklist to correct mistakes.

☐ Does each sentence add a new thought to your letter?

☐ Is every word or special term spelled correctly?

☐ Does each sentence begin with a capital letter and end with correct punctuation?

☐ Do all names begin with a capital letter?

☐ Could other words be used to give more detail?

Publishing Use this checklist to prepare for publication.

☐ Read your letter one more time. Make sure all of the parts of the letter are there.

☐ Write or type your letter.

☐ Sign your letter.

Name _____ Date _____

Three-Letter Consonant Blends

Focus
- A consonant blend is when two or more consonants are together in a word and each sound can be heard.
- Some common three-letter consonant blends are *str, scr, spr,* and *spl.*

Word List
1. straw
2. split
3. scrape
4. stretch
5. splash
6. scream
7. sprawl
8. sprout
9. strange
10. scratch

Challenge Words
11. strength
12. spry
13. screen

Practice **Sort the spelling words under the correct heading.**

str **blend**

1. _____
2. _____
3. _____

scr **blend**

4. _____
5. _____
6. _____

spr **blend**

7. _____
8. _____

spl **blend**

9. _____
10. _____

Apply **Visualization Strategy** Circle the correct spelling for each word. Then write the correct word on the line.

11. skrach   scratch   _____

12. strange   stiranj   _____

13. sprout   spurowt   _____

14. spullit   split   _____

15. scream   skreem   _____

Meaning Strategy Write the spelling word that best fits the sentence.

16. The dolphins made a big _____ at the end of their show.

17. We had to _____ the old paint off of the dresser before we could put on a new coat.

18. There were so many new buildings going up in the city that it began to _____ out to the countryside.

19. Could I please have a _____ for my drink?

20. The balloon began to _____ as it filled with air.

Name _____ **Date** _____

Use Multiple Sources

Write your investigation question and your conjecture.

_____

_____

_____

_____

_____

There are many different sources you can turn to for your investigation. Complete the questions below about two possible sources you could use.

First Source: _____

• What type of information does this source contain?

_____

• What might you learn from this source about your question?

_____

_____

_____

- Find the name of one source of this kind (in a library) that you might be able to use in your investigation.

_____

_____

Second Source: _____

_____

- What type of information does this source contain?

_____

_____

- What might you learn from this source?

_____

_____

- Find the name of one source of this kind (in a library) that you might be able to use in your investigation.

_____

_____

Name _____ Date _____

Capitalization and Noun Review

Focus
- There are many rules for **capitalization**. The following words must begin with a capital letter: **proper nouns, titles, initials, days, months, cities,** and **states**.
- A **singular noun** names one thing. A **plural noun** names more than one.

Practice **Read each sentence. Underline three times letters that should be capitalized.**

1. Every saturday my family likes to take a trip to highbanks park.

2. My friend j.d. was born in birmingham, alabama.

Write the plural form of each noun below. Remember spelling rules.

1. woman _____   **2.** wish _____

**Apply** **Write a sentence including the types of words in parentheses ( ).**

1. (title, singular noun) _____

_____

Adjectives and Articles Review

Focus

- An **adjective** is a word that describes a person, place, or thing.
- An **article** is a special kind of adjective. The three articles are: *a, an,* and *the.*
- Adjectives that **compare** two nouns or pronouns end in *–er*. Adjectives that compare more than two nouns or pronouns end in *–est*. The words *more* or *most* can also be used to compare adjectives.

Practice Circle the adjectives and underline the articles in each sentence.

1. The black bat and the blue whale are mammals.

2. Big elephants and little rats are mammals too.

3. All mammals have thick fur.

Apply Write a sentence including the types of words in parentheses ( ).

1. (adjective) _____

2. (article) _____

3. (comparative adjectives using -*er*) _____

_____

Name _____ Date _____

/ow/ and /aw/ Sounds/Spellings

Focus
- The /ow/ sound can be spelled **ow** and **ou_**.
- The /aw/ sound can be spelled **aw** and **au_**.

Practice Underline the /ow/ or /aw/ spelling pattern in each word. Write a rhyming word with the same spelling pattern. Underline the spelling pattern in the rhyming word.

1. frown _____   **4.** claw _____

2. Paul _____   **5.** now _____

3. sound _____

Read the clue and fill in the correct spelling pattern for each answer to complete the word.

1. a place to live   h_____se

2. circus performer   cl_____n

3. moving on your knees   cr_____l

4. a summer month   _____gust

5. a large hill   m_____ntain

6. a rule   l_____

Apply **Circle the correct word that completes the sentence.**

1. Missy looked for shapes in the _____.

   a. clowds   **b.** clouds   **c.** clauds

2. A kite was _____ in the tree's highest branches.

   a. caught   **b.** cowt   **c.** cawt

3. The daisy is my aunt's favorite _____.

   a. flouer   **b.** flauer   **c.** flower

4. My kitten has a hurt _____.

   a. paw   **b.** pau   **c.** pou

5. There was a long line at the water _____.

   a. fauntain   **b.** fountain   **c.** fowtain

6. The rocket was almost ready to _____.

   a. launch   **b.** lownch   **c.** lounch

7. I heard a coyote _____.

   a. hawl   **b.** houl   **c.** howl

8. What made that _____ noise?

   a. lowd   **b.** loud   **c.** lawd

Name _____ Date _____

Suffixes: –ly, –y, –less, and –ful

Focus

- A **suffix** is added to the end of a base word. Adding a suffix changes the meaning of the word.
- The **suffix –ly** means *"in a certain way."*
- The **suffix –y** means *"full of."*
- The **suffix –less** means *"without."*
- The **suffix –ful** means *"full of."*

Practice Choose a suffix from above to add to each base word that will make sense. Write the meaning of the new word.

1. flaw_____   _____

2. thirst_____   _____

3. fond_____   _____

4. youth_____   _____

Write two sentences using two of the words above.

1. –ly   _____

2. –y   _____

Apply Choose one of the following suffixes to add to the base word in parentheses ( ) that will complete the sentence. Write the new word on the blank line. Write the meaning of the new word.

–ly	–y	–less	–ful

1. Don't be _____ (care) when carrying the glass vase.

New Meaning: _____

2. I get scared when it is _____ (storm) outside.

New Meaning: _____

3. Spread the peanut butter _____ (even) on the bread.

New Meaning: _____

4. We said a _____ (tear) good-bye at the airport.

New Meaning: _____

5. The autumn air is sometimes _____ (chill).

New Meaning: _____

6. Wendy _____ (sudden) dropped her book.

New Meaning: _____

Name _____ Date _____

Selection Vocabulary

Focus

calves *n.* Plural of **calf:** the back part of the lower leg.

shuffled *v.* Past tense of **shuffle:** to drag one's feet while walking.

glimpse *n.* A quick view.

pounding *v.* Beating.

strolled *v.* Past tense of **stroll:** to walk in a slow, relaxed way.

slipped *v.* Past tense of **slip:** to put on.

ached *v.* Past tense of **ache:** to hurt with a dull steady pain.

pale *adj.* Light in color.

Practice **Write the word that best matches the underlined word or phrase in the sentences below.**

1. The <u>backs of my legs</u> hurt from running so much.

_____

2. Annie's heart was <u>beating</u> very fast with excitement.

_____

3. Our kitchen is a <u>light color</u>. _____

4. I was only able to get a <u>quick view</u> of the dress.

_____

Apply Get a partner and take turns acting out each of the vocabulary words. You do not have to go in order. Put a check by the words your partner was able to guess correctly and an X by the words they could not guess correctly.

1. calves   **5.** shuffled

2. glimpse   **6.** pounding

3. strolled   **7.** slipped

4. pale   **8.** ached

Which word was the easiest to act out?

_____

Why? _____

Which word was the most difficult to act out?

_____

Why? _____

Writing a Realistic Story

Think

Audience: Who will read your story?

_____

Purpose: What is your reason for writing your story?

_____

Prewriting
Decide on your main character. Write the character's name on the top line. Write a list of details about your main character.

Main Character: _____

Details: _____

Fill in the details on the story map.

Characters:
Setting:

PLOT

Beginning:
Middle:
End:

Narrator of the story (point of view):

Revising Use this checklist to revise.

- ☐ Are your characters and setting realistic?

- ☐ Could the events in your story really happen?

- ☐ Will your reader be able to follow your story?

- ☐ Did you use dialogue to show how your characters think and feel?

Editing/Proofreading Use this checklist to correct mistakes.

- ☐ Is every word or special term spelled correctly?

- ☐ Did you use correct punctuation in dialogue?

- ☐ Does every sentence start with a capital letter and end with correct punctuation?

- ☐ Can you add details to make your story more exciting and realistic?

Publishing Use this checklist to prepare for publication.

- ☐ Give your story a title.

- ☐ Write or type a neat copy.

- ☐ Include a drawing that shows a character or event from your story.

Name _____ **Date** _____

Contrast Sound/Spellings for /aw/ and /ow/

Focus
- The **/aw/** sound sounds like the word lawn.
- Two ways the **/aw/** sound can be spelled are aw and au_.
- The **/ow/** sound sounds like the word brown.
- It can be spelled ow and ou_.

Practice **Sort the spelling words under the correct heading.**

/aw/ spelled *aw*

1. _____
2. _____
3. _____
4. _____

/aw/ spelled *au*

5. _____

/aw/ spelled *ow*

6. _____
7. _____
8. _____
9. _____

/aw/ spelled *ou*

10. _____

Word List
1. tawny
2. tower
3. pause
4. pounding
5. shawl
6. shower
7. claw
8. clown
9. awe
10. owl

Challenge Words
11. applaud
12. awkward

Skills Practice 2 • Spelling

Apply **Rhyming Strategy** Write the spelling word or words that rhyme with each pair of words below.

11. power   flower   _____ _____

12. draw   saw   _____

13. down   town   _____

14. brawny   scrawny   _____

15. fowl   growl   _____

16. crawl   sprawl   _____

Meaning Strategy Fill in the blank with the spelling word that best completes the sentence. One word will be used twice in the same sentence.

pause	pounding	awe

17. The sound of a _____ hammer can sometimes

give you a _____ headache.

18. TV shows have to _____ for commercials.

19. I was in _____ of how tall the Washington

Monument was.

Name _____ Date _____

Study Skills

Focus Using Newspapers and Magazines

Practice Find a story or article in a newspaper or a magazine that is related to your unit investigation. Then answer the questions below.

Is your article from a newspaper or a magazine?

_____

_____

What is the name and date of the magazine or newspaper?

_____

_____

What is the name of the article?

_____

_____

What is the article about?

_____

_____

How does the article help you with your unit investigation?

_____

_____

Name _____ Date _____

Subject/Verb Agreement and Commas in a Series Review

Focus
- The **subject** and **verb** in a sentence must agree. The subject and verb must both be singular, or both must be plural.
- A **comma** is used after each item in a series or list of things except the last one.

Practice **Circle the sentence that has the commas in the right places.**

1. a. Cars can be red, blue, black, or green.

   b. Cars can be red blue, black, or green, .

2. a. Are football, basketball, and baseball, alike?

   b. Are football, basketball, and baseball alike?

Circle the sentence that has subject and verb agreement.

1. a. A house plant grows indoors.

   b. House plants grows indoors.

2. a. Leaf change color in the fall.

   b. Leaves change color in the fall.

Possessive Nouns/Pronouns and Contractions Review

Focus
- A **possessive noun** ends in an apostrophe s or just an apostrophe (').
- A **possessive pronoun** takes the place of a possessive noun.
- A **contraction** puts two words together. An apostrophe takes the place of the letters taken out.

Practice Circle the possessive noun or pronoun and underline the contraction in each sentence.

1. Jamie's mom can't make it to dinner tonight.

2. Shouldn't our car get fixed today?

Apply Write a sentence using a contraction.

1. _____

Write a sentence using a noun and pronoun that agree in number and gender.

1. _____

Name _____ Date _____

/aw/, /ow/, /o͞o/, /oo/, /ū/ and /ō/ Sounds/Spellings, Silent Letters, and Three-Letter Blends Review

Focus

- The **ow** spelling pattern can make the /ō/ sound or the /ow/ sound.

- The **u, u_e, _ue**, and **_ew** spelling patterns can make the /o͞o/ and /ū/ sounds.

- The **oo** spelling pattern can make the /o͞o/ and /oo/ sounds.

- The **ow** and **ou_** spelling patterns can make the /ow/ sound.

- The **aw** and **au_** spelling patterns can make the /aw/ sound.

Practice Circle the spelling pattern in each word below. Write the sound each word makes: /aw/, /ow/, /oo/, /o͞o/, /ō/, or /ū/.

1. straw _____

2. burrow _____

3. hoof _____

4. boost _____

5. counting _____

6. screw _____

Silent Letters and Three-Letter Blends Review

Focus
- **Silent letters** in a word are not heard when the word is read.
- **str   scr   spl   spr**

The sounds of these letters often combine at the beginning of words. We say the three sounds quickly without any space between them.

Practice Read each word below. Circle a three letter blend or silent letter that is in each word. Identify the spelling pattern circled by writing blend or silent letter.

1. tomb _____

2. stroke _____

3. scramble _____

4. writer _____

Apply Use one of the following words to fill in each blank.

strawberry	spray
knot	stripe

1. Hannah had a _____ in her shoelace.

2. Be sure to put on bug _____ before camping.

3. A skunk has a white _____ down its tail.

4. _____ pie is my favorite dessert.

Name _____ Date _____

Homophones and Homographs

Focus
- **Homophones** are words that are pronounced the same but spelled differently and have different meanings.
- **Homographs** are words that are spelled and pronounced the same but have different meanings.

Practice Write the word from the box that is the homophone of each word below.

piece	two	see	fourth	rode

1. peace _____

3. forth _____

2. sea _____

4. to _____

Circle the word in each pair that is a homograph.

1. watch   cup

3. punch   found

2. door   sink

4. school   ball

Apply Use a pair of homophones from above to complete the sentence.

1. It was easy to _____ the _____ from our house.

Skills Practice 2 • Word Structure

Related Words and Word Families

Focus
- Knowing how words are **related** can help readers figure out the meaning of words.
- A **base word** can give a clue to the meaning of other words in the word family.

Practice **Write the three words in order to show a relationship. Write an explanation of the relationship. The first one has been done for you.**

1. flower   plant   rose
plant   flower   rose
A rose is a type of flower. A flower is a type of plant.

2. grocery   building   store

_____ _____ _____

_____

3. convertible   car   transportation

_____ _____ _____

_____

Write the base word for each word family.

1. walk, walking, walks _____ **2.** stars, starfish, starlight _____

Name _____   Date _____

Selection Vocabulary

Focus

treated *v.* Past tense of **treat**: to behave toward or deal with in a certain way.

crops *n.* Plural of **crop**: fruits, vegetables, or other plants that are grown on a farm and sold.

union *n.* A group of workers who join together to get better pay and working conditions.

boycott *v.* To refuse to buy something until workers are treated better.

border *n.* A line where one country or other area ends and another begins.

weakened *v.* Past tense of **weaken**: to grow less strong.

strike *v.* To stop work in order to get better pay and working conditions.

awarded *v.* Past tense of **award**: to give a prize.

Practice   Write four sentences that use at least one vocabulary word from this lesson.

1. _____

2. _____

3. _____

4. _____

Apply   **Use the vocabulary words to complete each sentence.**

1. In the 1880's Cesar Chavez crossed the

_____ into Texas.

2. Cesar Chavez believed workers should be

_____ fairly.

3. He helped farm workers to come together and form

a _____.

4. During the Great Depression, the family worked

picking _____.

5. In 1965 grape pickers went on _____

and wanted a _____ of buying grapes.

6. Going on hunger strikes must have

_____ him.

7. Cesar Chavez was _____ the
Medal of Freedom.

Name _____ Date _____

Drawing Conclusions

Focus
- Thinking about the information in a story can help readers make decisions about what is happening.
- Readers can **draw conclusions** about a character or event in a story by using information in the story's words and pictures.

Practice **Read the following paragraph. Then answer the questions below by drawing conclusions.**

Our teacher, Ms. Smith, began talking to herself. "Now, where are they? I can't read without them." She looked through her desk drawers. She looked in her purse. She patted her pockets. As Ms. Smith scratched her head, we began to giggle. She found what she had been looking for. "I always leave them up there," she laughed.

What was Ms. Smith doing? _____

Why did the students giggle when Ms. Smith scratched her head?

_____

Write one clue that lets you know she was looking for her *glasses*.

1. _____

Apply **Read the following pages of "Cesar Chavez".
Draw one conclusion after reading and write it
down. Write down one sentence from the text that helped you
draw your conclusion.**

1. pg. 401

Conclusion: _____

Supporting Sentence: _____

_____

2. pg. 406

Conclusion: _____

Supporting Sentence: _____

_____

3. pg. 411

Conclusion: _____

Supporting Sentence: _____

_____

Name _____ **Date** _____

Writing a Biography

 **Think** **Audience: Who** will read your biography?

_____

Purpose: What is your reason for writing a biography?

_____

Prewriting **Use this graphic organizer to record the main idea and details of your biography.**

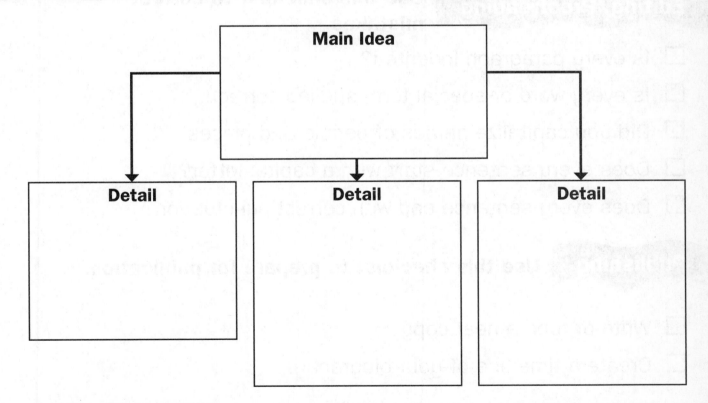

On a separate sheet of paper write at least three important dates and the event for each date from the person's life.

Revising Use this checklist to revise.

☐ Is the main idea in the first paragraph?

☐ Do your details support the main idea?

☐ Are the events in the proper sequence and do they flow from one event to the next?

☐ Did you leave out any important dates or events?

☐ Did you use clear, specific words that tell where, when, and how things happened?

Editing/Proofreading Use this checklist to correct mistakes.

☐ Is every paragraph indented?

☐ Is every word or special term spelled correctly?

☐ Did you capitalize names of people and places?

☐ Does every sentence start with a capital letter?

☐ Does every sentence end with correct punctuation?

Publishing Use this checklist to prepare for publication.

☐ Write or type a neat copy.

☐ Create a time line of your biography.

Name _____ **Date** _____

Review: Lessons 1-4

Focus
- The *oo* spelling makes different sounds. One sound is **/oo/,** as in the word *cook.*
- Another sound is **/o͞o/,** as in the word *root.*
- One spelling for the **/aw/** sound is *aw,* as in the word *crawl.*
- The *ow* spelling can make the sound of /ō/, as in the word *row.* It can also make the **/ow/** sound, as in the word *cow.*
- Three-letter consonant blends are when three consonants are together in a word and each consonant keeps its own sound when pronounced, as in the word *straw.*

Word List
1. law
2. low
3. boot
4. book
5. doom
6. took
7. allow
8. arrow
9. string
10. spring

Challenge Words
11. describe
12. strict

Practice Sort the spelling words under the correct heading.

ow as in *flow*

1. _____

2. _____

ow as in *now*

3. _____

/oo/ sound

4. _____

5. _____

/o͞o/ sound

6. _____

7. _____

/aw/ sound

8. _____

Three-letter consonant blends

9. _____

10. _____

Apply **Rhyming Strategy** Write the spelling word or words that rhyme with each word or pair of words below.

1. cook   look   _____ _____

2. room   gloom   _____

3. claw   jaw   _____

4. crow   slow   _____

5. bring   sing   _____ _____

Visualization Strategy Read each pair of words below. Circle the correctly spelled word. Then write the correctly spelled word on the line.

1. bute   boot   _____

2. ulou   allow   _____

3. door   dore   _____

4. arrow   airo   _____

Name _____ **Date** _____

Using New Technology

After you have conducted your investigation, you could use a form of technology—such as a computer, a video camera, or a color printer—to present your information.

Complete the questions below about using a form of new technology to help present information.

• First Idea for a Presentation

What would be one way to present your information without using new technology?

_____

_____

_____

_____

How could you use a form of new technology to help you present the same information?

_____

_____

_____

_____

• Second Idea for a Presentation

What would be another way to present your information
without using new technology?

_____

_____

_____

_____

How could you use a form of new technology to help
you present the same information?

_____

_____

_____

_____

Name _____ Date _____

Compound and Imperative Sentences Review

Focus
- A **compound sentence** is made when two sentences with similar ideas are combined into one sentence.

- A **conjunction** is a word that connects words or ideas. *And, or*, and *but* are conjunctions.

- An **imperative sentence** gives a command and ends in a period.

Practice **Read each sentence. Write C for a compound sentence or I for an imperative sentence.**
Underline the conjunction in each compound sentence.

1. Clean the kitchen and dining room. _____

2. Gail has a dog and she has two cats. _____

3. Open your books to page three. _____

Apply **Write an imperative sentence.**

1. _____

Write a compound sentence. Underline the conjunction.

1. _____

Colons, Synonyms, and Antonyms Review

Focus
- A **colon** is used to introduce a list and to separate the hour from the minutes when you write the time.
- **Synonyms** are words that are similar in meaning.
- **Antonyms** are words that are opposite in meaning.

Practice **Write the following times using a colon correctly.**

1. two-fifteen _____

2. three o'clock _____

3. six thirty _____

4. nine forty-five _____

Circle the two words in each row that go together. Write synonym or antonym to describe each pair of words.

1. friendly   talk   see   nice   _____

2. light   found   lost   dig   _____

Apply **Write a sentence that includes a list of items. Use colons and commas correctly.**

1. _____

Write a pair of synonyms and a pair of antonyms.

Synonyms	Antonyms
1. _____ _____	**2.** _____ _____